Ninja Foodi Smart XL Grill Cookbook for Beginners

Easy & Delicious Indoor Grilling and Air Frying Recipes

for Your Party, Holiday, and Daily Diet

Kimberly Hackler

© Copyright 2020 - All rights reserved.

No part of this publication may be reproduced, distributed, or transmitted in any form or by any means, including photocopying, recording, or other electronic or mechanical methods, without the prior written permission of the publisher, except in the case of brief quotations embodied in reviews and certain other non-commercial uses permitted by copyright law.

This Book is provided with the sole purpose of providing relevant information on a specific topic for which every reasonable effort has been made to ensure that it is both accurate and reasonable. Nevertheless, by purchasing this Book you consent to the fact that the author, as well as the publisher, are in no way experts on the topics contained herein, regardless of any claims as such that may be made within. It is recommended that you always consult a professional prior to undertaking any of the advice or techniques discussed within. This is a legally binding declaration that is considered both valid and fair by both the Committee of Publishers Association and the American Bar Association and should be considered as legally binding within the United States.

Table of Contents

Chapter 1: The Ninja Foodi Smart XL Grill 5

What is the Ninja Foodi Smart XL Grill? 5

Functions and Buttons of the Ninja Foodi Smart XL Grill 5

Common mistakes that you might make .. 7

General Tips and FAQ's 7

How to Clean and Maintain Your Ninja Foodi Smart XL Grill? 9

Chapter 2: Breakfast Recipes 10

Awesome Tater Tots Eggs 10

Avocado Flautas 11

French Morning Toasties 12

Bacon Bombs 12

Juicy Stuffed Bell Peppers 13

Mushroom Pepper Meal 14

Breakfast Pockets 15

Energetic Bagel Platter 16

Classic French Burrito 17

Sweet BBQ Chicken Meal 17

Chapter 3: Chicken and Poultry Recipes .. 19

Easy Turkey Cutlets 19

Greek Chicken Breasts 20

Meatballs 21

Simple Parmesan Chicken Breast 22

Italian Parmesan Chicken Breast 23

Crispy Chicken Breast 24

Flovrful Chicken Drumsticks 25

Sweet & Spicy Chicken 26

Simple Baked Chicken Breasts 27

Easy Chicken Fajita 28

Tasty Parmesan Chicken Wings 29

Lemon Pepper Chicken 30

Flavorful & Juicy Grilled Chicken 31

Meatballs 32

Crispy Chicken Wings 33

Chapter 4: Meat Recipes 34

Spicy Baked Pork Chops 34

Rosemary Lamb Chops 35

Baked Lamb Patties 36

Garlic Butter Steak 37

Air Fry Sausage Balls 38

Asian Short Ribs 39

Air Fry Sirloin Steak 40

Meatballs 41

Meatballs 42

Easy Montreal Seasoned Steak 43

Easy Burger Patty 44

Sweet & Savory Pork Chops 45

Marinated Pork Chops 46

Delicious Beef Patties 47

Flavorful Marinated Steak 48

Chapter 5: Snacks Recipes 49

Basil Pizzas 49

Seared Tuna Salad 50

Fajita Skewers 51
Lemon-Garlic Shrimp Caesar Salad 52
Crispy Rosemary Potatoes 53
Honey Mustard Chicken Tenders 54
Portobello and Pesto Sliders 55
Bacon Brussels Delight 56
Juicy Honey Carrots 57
Seasoned Broccoli Dish 58
Spicy Barbecue Chicken Drumsticks 59
Simple Crispy Brussels 60
Cajun Eggplant Appetizer 61
Grilled Eggplant, Tomato and Mozzarella Stacks 62
Honey Asparagus 63
Crispy Potato Cubes 64
Healthy Onion Rings 65

Chapter 6: Fish and Seafood Recipes 66

Juicy Lemon and Mustard Fish 66
The Cool Haddock Bake 67
Southern Catfish 68
Garlic and Salmon Extravaganza 69
Broiled Tilapia 70
Paprika Shrimp 71
Salmon and Broccoli 72
Air Crisped Salmon 73
Breaded Shrimp 74
Tuna Patties 75
Excellent Clams 76
Crispy Healthy Crabby Patties 77
Butter and Garlic Shrimp 78

4 Ingredients Catfish 79
Shrimp Lettuce Wraps 80

Chapter 7: Vegetarian and Vegan Recipes 81

Spiced Up Chickpeas 81
Cheesy Zucchini Love 82
Hyper Garlic Potatoes 83
Fancy Asparagus and Roasted Potatoes . 84
Mexican Corn Dish 85
Tomatoes Balsamic Roast 86
Lemon Pepper Brussels Sprouts 86
Spicy Broccoli Medley 87
Feisty Avocado Toast 88

Chapter 8: Desserts Recipes 89

Grilled Honey Carrots 89
Amazing Fried Tomatoes 90
Cheesed Up Cauliflower Steak 91
Cherry Choco Bars 92
Amazing Blueberry Cobbler 93
Corn Bread Biscuits 94
Feisty Rum and Pineapple Sundae 95
Marshmallow and Banana Boats 96
Blueberry Lemon Muffins 96
Baked Apple 97
Fruity Lime Salad 98
Banana Fritter 99
Mozzarella Sticks and Grilled Eggplant .. 100
Granola Muffins 101
Cinnamon Sugar Roasted Chickpeas 102

Chapter 1: The Ninja Foodi Smart XL Grill

What is the Ninja Foodi Smart XL Grill?

The introduction of "Smart" technology in almost every domain and aspect of life has changed modern-day man's lifestyle. The cooking world has also been impacted vastly with the introduction of the Ninja Foodi Smart XL Grill. The reason is that it provides you with crucial cooking techniques like pressure cooking, grilling, air crisping, searing, broiling, sautéing, dehydrating, and grilling, etc. all in one single device. It is the reason why it is going to replace many conventional cooking appliances in your kitchen and provide you with a Smart, single solution to all your cooking modes. The best thing about the Ninja Foodi Smart XL Grill is that it can be used both indoor as well as outdoor while being on camping or family picnics. Moreover, it is certified as a smoke-free device providing you with the most convenient possible.

The Ninja Foodi Smart XL Grill preserves the natural taste of the ingredients and gives a fresh aroma to your food. It helps you maintain the natural flavor, as well as the nutrition of the ingredients involved in the recipe of your food. Furthermore, it also comes with a kitchen thermometer, which is super beneficial in giving your food the right and most suitable cooking temperature. This correct temperature range is useful in giving your food the perfect and the right tenderness and crispiness. As a whole, the Ninja Foodi Smart XL Grill is considered to be one of the significant breakthroughs in the cooking world. It can be clearly referred to as the one ultimate choice for every single one of your cooking modes. The Ninja Foodi Smart XL Grill comes with various features and functions that make it stand ahead from the rest of its competitors.

Functions and Buttons of the Ninja Foodi Smart XL Grill

Now that you have a basic idea of what the Ninja Foodi Smart XL Grill is, let's have a look at the core functions and buttons that you should know about. Keep in mind that you have five different types of cooking that you can do using your Ninja Foodi Grill.

Grill

At its heart, the Ninja Foodi Smart XL Grill is an indoor grill, so to unlock its full potential, you must have a good understanding of how the grill function of the appliance works, so let me break it down to you.

Now you should understand that each set of the Grill is specifically designed for different types of food.

But regardless of which function you choose, the first step for you will always be

Place your cooking pot and grill grate in the Ninja Foodi

Let it pre-heat

Then add your food

The next thing would be to select the Grill function and choose the Grill Temperature, here you have 4 settings to choose from.

Low: This mode is perfect for bacon and sausages.

Medium: This is perfect for frozen meats or marinated meats.

High: This mode is perfect for steaks, chicken, and burgers.

Max: This is perfect for vegetables, fruits, fresh and frozen seafood, and pizza.

Bake

As mentioned earlier, the Ninja Foodi Smart XL Grill is essentially a mini convection oven. All you need to bake bread, cakes, pies, and other sweet treats is a Cooking Pot and this function. The Pre-heat time for the Bake mode is just 3 minutes.

Air Crisp

The Air Crisp mode will help you to achieve a very crispy and crunchy golden brown finish to your food. Using the Air Crisp mode combined with the crisper basket is the perfect combination to cook your frozen foods such as French Fries, Onion rings, Chicken Nuggets, etc.

Air Crisp is also amazing for Brussels Sprouts and other fresh vegetables. Just always make sure to shake the crisper basket once or twice to ensure even cooking.

Dehydrate

Generally speaking, Dehydrators are pretty expensive and take a lot of space in your kitchen. Luckily, using the Dehydrate function, you can very easily dehydrate fruits, meats, vegetables, herbs, etc. using just your Ninja Foodi Grill!

Roast

The Roast function is used to make everything from slow-roasted pot roast to appetizers to casual sides. Large pieces of protein can be put directly in your Ninja Foodi Smart XL Grill and roasted using this function. You can further make this mode more effective by using a Roasting Rack accessory.

Common mistakes that you might make

As a new user of the Ninja Foodi Grill, there are certain mistakes that you might make. You must know some of the most common ones so that you can avoid making them during your early days.

Always make sure to give enough time to your Ninja Foodi Smart XL Grill to let it pre-heat. Pre-heating the appliance will bring the internal temperature to an optimum level and you will get the best results possible.

Some people might think that it is not possible to grill or cook vegetables in the Ninja Foodi Grill, don't make that mistake! Make sure to cook your veggies as well!

The Ninja Foodi Smart XL Grill is best for when you are making recipes from scratch, don't try to add ingredients that are already cooked or fried.

If you overcrowd the cooking basket, the ingredients won't get enough space and as a result, the appliance won't be able to circulate heated air all around it properly, resulting in uneven cooking. So cook in batches if needed, but always make sure to keep spaces in between.

When you own a grilling appliance, baking doesn't come first to mind! But it is very much possible to bake goods in your Ninja Foodi Grill, so give it a try!

While using the Ninja Foodi Grill, some people often try to cook meals without using any oil at all! That is not ideal. You should keep in mind that a minimum of 1 to 2 teaspoons of oil is needed to cook meals properly, while 1-2 tablespoons are needed for breaded items.

You must learn how to properly cook the Ninja Foodi Grill, otherwise, you might end up damaging the appliance. Make sure to go through the section titled "How To Clean And Ninja Foodi Grill?" to properly learn how to.

General Tips and FAQ's

General Tips

Below are some tips that might help you to further enhance your grilling experience and ensure that you come up with the best possible grilled result possible!

Always make sure to give your appliance enough time to pre-heat before starting to cook your meals.

You must use a bit of oil while cooking. Brushing your vegetables and meats with a bit of oil helps to promote charring and crisping. If you want less smoke, then try to go for oil with high smoke point such as canola oil, avocado oil, etc.

Once you are ready to put food into your appliance, make sure to evenly arrange them well keeping a good amount of space between them to ensure even charring.

If you are worried about burning your food, you can always lift the hood to check the condition of your food. The Ninja Foodi Smart XL Grill automatically pauses the cooking process when you lift it and start again once you close it.

Always make sure to season your protein generously and let them sit at room temperature for at least 30 minutes. It will not only infuse flavors but will promote faster cooking as well.

Always try to keep a meat thermometer handy so that you can check your meat for doneness.

FAQ's

If this is your first time using the Ninja Foodi Grill, then naturally you might have some questions. Below are some of the most common ones that you might want to know about:

Q1. Why is my food burned?

You should understand the no two proteins are ever the same and for that very reason, the time taken to cook them will be different as well. Always make sure to pay very close attention to the size of the meat as well as the shape, as they play a huge role in the time taken for them to cook. Some sizes may require you to lower time while others may need you to increase the time. For the best result, always make sure to check the meat for doneness while it is cooking (use a meat thermometer if needed).

Q2. Can I Cook Frozen Food in Ninja Foodi Grill?

Yes, one of the best features of the Ninja Foodi Smart XL Grill is that you can cook frozen food straight out of the fridge without waiting for them defrost!

Q3. Can I Crisp Air battered ingredients?

Yes, it is possible to do that, however, you should use the proper breading technique. It is very much important to keep in mind that you coat your food first with flour ad then with egg and lastly with breadcrumbs. Finally, always make sure to press the bread crumbs onto the protein to ensure that they stick well. And lastly, make sure to spray some oil in order.

Q4. How long should I pre-heated the Ninja Foodi Grill?

The Ninja Foodi Smart XL Grill has a temperature-sensitive Grill Grate so that it can monitor the temperature while cooking. It is essential that you always let the appliance pre-heat before adding your ingredients, generally speaking, the Grill function takes about 8 minutes to preheat. Once the appliance is heated, it will let you know with a "Beep" sound. You can easily track the progress by waiting for the beep or looking at the indicator on the control panel. Once the Ninja Foodi Smart XL Grill is heated, it will also show "Add Food" denoting that it is not alright to add food.

Clean and Maintain Ninja Foodi Smart XL Grill

It might appear very tricky to thoroughly clean the Ninja Foodi Smart XL Grill, but it is not complicated at all. You merely need to follow certain easy steps, and your device is ready to go for another round. It is recommended to thoroughly clean the Ninja Foodi Smart XL Grill after every use. To clean the unit thoroughly and safely, follow the following guidelines:

- Let the device cool down before cleaning.
- Unplug the device from the power source.
- For quick cooling, keep the hood of the device open.
- The grill gate, splatter shield, crisper basket, cooking pot, cleaning brush, and the rest of the accessories are certified as **DISHWASHER SAFE**.
- The thermometer is not dishwasher safe.
- Rinse the accessories like splatter shield, grill gate, etc. for better cleaning results.
- Use the cleaning brush included with the device for handwashing.
- For cleaning baked-on cheese or sauces, utilize the other end of the cleaning brush for being used as a scrapper for effective hand washing.
- Either towel-dry or air-dry all the components after hand washing.
- **DO NOT** dip the main unit in any liquid, including water.
- **DO NOT** use any rasping cleaners or tools.
- **NEVER** use any sort of liquid cleaning solution near or on the thermometer.
- Always use a cotton swab or compressed air to avoid any damage to the jack.

In case of any grease or food residue left and stuck on the components of the Ninja Foodi Smart XL Grill, follow the following cleaning steps thoroughly:

1. If the residue is stuck on the splatter shield, grill gate, or any other accessory or part, soak it in warm soapy water solution before cleaning.

2. The splatter should be cleaned thoroughly after every use. For better cleansing, soak it in warm water overnight will assists efficiently in softening the stuck grease or sauces.

3. You can also deep clean the splatter shield by thoroughly immersing it in water and further boiling it for approximately 10 minutes.

4. Moreover, you can then rinse it effectively with room temperature water and let it dry properly for better results.

For deep cleaning the thermometer, you can soak both the silicone grip and the stainless steel tip in a container full of warm water. But, keep in mind that the jack or the cord **SHOULD NOT** be immersed or soaked in any solution, including water, as mentioned earlier. The thermometer holder of the Ninja Foodi Smart XL Grill is clearly **HANDWASH** only.

Chapter 2: Breakfast Recipes

Awesome Tater Tots Eggs

Prepping time: 5-10 minutes/ Cooking time: 25 minutes /For 4 servings

Ingredients

- 1 pound frozen tater tots
- 1 cup cheddar cheese, shredded
- 2 sausages, cooked and sliced
- Cooking spray as needed
- Salt and pepper to taste
- ¼ cup milk
- 5 whole eggs

Directions

1. Preheat your Ninja Foodi Smart XL in Bake mode at 390 degrees F for 3 minutes
2. Take a bowl and add eggs, milk, season with salt and pepper
3. Take a small baking pan and grease with oil
4. Add egg mix to the pan and transfer to your Foodi
5. Cook for 5 minutes, place sausages on top of eggs, sprinkle cheese on top
6. Bake for 20 minutes more
7. Serve and enjoy!

Nutrition value per serving

Calories: 187, Fat: 8 g, Saturated Fat: 3 g, Carbohydrates: 21 g, Fiber: 1 g, Sodium: 338 mg, Protein: 9 g

Avocado Flautas

Prepping time: 5minutes/ Cooking time: 15 minutes /For 8 servings

Ingredients

- 8 eggs, beaten
- 1 tablespoon butter
- ½ teaspoon salt
- 1½ teaspoons cumin
- 8 fajita size tortillas
- 8 bacon slices, cooked
- ½ cup feta cheese, crumbled
- ¼ teaspoon pepper
- 1 teaspoon chili powder
- 4 oz cream cheese, softened
- ½ cup Mexican cheese, shredded

AVOCADO CRÈME

- ½ cup sour cream
- ½ teaspoon salt
- 2 small avocados
- 1 lime, juiced
- ¼ teaspoon black pepper

Directions

1. Press the "Air Crisp" button on the Ninja Foodi Smart XL Grill and adjust the time for 10 minutes at 400 degrees F.
2. Put butter in a skillet on medium heat and add eggs.
3. Stir fry for 3 minutes and add salt, chili powder, pepper, and cumin.
4. Spread cream cheese on the tortillas and place bacon pieces over them.
5. Top with egg mixture and shredded cheese.
6. Tightly roll each tortilla and place them in the Ninja Foodi when it shows "Add Food".
7. Air crisp for 12 minutes, flipping halfway through.
8. Put the avocado crème ingredients in a blender and process until smooth.
9. Dish out the baked flautas in a platter and serve warm with avocado cheese and cotija cheese.

Nutrition value per serving

Calories: 212, Fat: 11.8g, Saturated Fat: 2.2g, Carbohydrates: 14.6g, Fiber: 4.4g, Sodium: 321mg, Protein: 17.3g

French Morning Toasties

Prepping time: 5-10 minutes/ Cooking time: 10 minutes /For 4 servings

Ingredients

- Cooking spray as needed
- 6 slices bread, sliced into strips
- ¼ teaspoon vanilla extract
- ¼ teaspoon ground cinnamon
- ¼ cup granulated sugar
- ½ cup milk
- 4 whole eggs

Directions

1. Take a bowl and beat in eggs, milk
2. Stir in sugar, vanilla, and cinnamon
3. Dip the bread in the mix
4. Preheat your Ninja Foodi Smart XL in AIR CRISP for 10 minutes at 400 degrees F
5. Transfer bread to the Foodi and cook for 3-5 minutes per side
6. Enjoy!

Nutrition value per serving

Calories: 183, Fat: 6 g, Saturated Fat: 2 g, Carbohydrates: 24 g, Fiber: 3 g, Sodium: 269 mg, Protein: 9 g

Bacon Bombs

Prepping time: 5minutes\ Cooking time: 7 minutes /For 4 servings

Ingredients

- 3 large eggs, lightly beaten
- 4-ounces whole-wheat pizza dough, freshly prepared
- Cooking spray

- 3 bacon slices, crisped and crumbled
- ounce cream cheese softened
- 1 tablespoon fresh chives, chopped

Directions

1. Press the "Bake" button on the Ninja Foodi Smart XL Grill and adjust the time for 16 minutes at 350 degrees F.
2. Crack eggs in a non-stick pan and stir fry for 1 minute.
3. Stir in the bacon, chives, and cream cheese and keep aside.
4. Cut the pizza dough into 4 equal pieces and roll each into circles.
5. Put ¼ of the bacon-egg mixture in the center of the dough circle and seal the edges with water.
6. Place the doughs in the Ninja Foodi when it shows "Add Food" and spray them with cooking oil.
7. Bake for 6 minutes and dish out to serve warm.

Nutrition value per serving

Calories: 284Fat: 7.9g, Saturated Fat: 0g, Carbohydrates: 46g, Fiber: 3.6g, Sodium: 704mg, Protein: 7.9g

Juicy Stuffed Bell Peppers

Prepping time: 10 minutes/ Cooking time:15 minutes /For 4 servings

Ingredients

- 4 slices bacon, cooked and chopped
- 4 large eggs
- 1 cup cheddar cheese, shredded
- 4 bell peppers, seeded and tops removed
- Chopped parsley for garnish
- Salt and pepper to taste

Directions

1. Divide cheese and bacon equally and stuff into your bell pepper
2. Add eggs into each bell pepper
3. Season with salt and pepper
4. Pre-heat your Ninja Foodi by pressing the "AIR CRISP" option and setting it to "390 Degrees F."
5. Set the timer to 15 minutes
6. Let it pre-heat until you hear a beep
7. Transfer bell pepper to your cooking basket and transfer to Ninja Foodi Grill
8. Lock lid and cook for 10-15 minutes
9. Cook until egg whites are cooked well until the yolks are slightly runny
10. Remove peppers from the basket and garnish with parsley
11. Serve and enjoy!

Nutrition value per serving

Calories: 326, Fat: 23 g, Saturated Fat: 10 g, Carbohydrates: 10 g, Fiber: 2 g, Sodium: 781 mg, Protein: 22 g

Mushroom Pepper Meal

Prepping time: 10 minutes/ Cooking time:10 minutes /For 4 servings

Ingredients

- 4 cremini mushrooms, sliced
- 4 large eggs
- ½ cup cheddar cheese, shredded
- ½ onion, chopped
- ¼ cup whole milk
- Sea salt
- ½ bell pepper, seeded and diced
- Black pepper

Directions

1. Add eggs and milk into a medium bowl
2. Whisk them together
3. Add mushrooms, onion, bell pepper, and cheese
4. Mix them well
5. Preheat by selecting the "BAKE" option and setting it to 400 degrees F
6. Set the timer for 10 minutes
7. Pour the egg mixture into the baking pan and spread evenly
8. Let it pre-heat until you hear a beep
9. Then close the lid
10. Cook for 10 minutes
11. Serve and enjoy!

Nutrition value per serving

Calories: 153, Fat: 10 g, Saturated Fat: 2 g, Carbohydrates: 5 g, Fiber: 1 g, Sodium: 494 mg, Protein: 11 g

Breakfast Pockets

Prepping time: 5minutes/ Cooking time: 11 minutes /For 6 servings

Ingredients

- 1 box puff pastry sheets
- 5 eggs
- ½ cup sausage crumbles, cooked
- ½ cup bacon, cooked
- ½ cup cheddar cheese, shredded

Directions

1. Press the "Bake" button on the Ninja Foodi Smart XL Grill and adjust the time for 10 minutes at 370 degrees F.
2. Crack eggs in a non-stick pan and stir fry for 1 minute.
3. Stir in the bacon and sausages and keep aside.

4. Cut the puff pastry into equal-sized rectangles and add a scoop of egg mixture and cheese in the center.

5. Seal the edges with water and transfer into the Ninja Foodi when it shows "Add Food."

6. Spray them with cooking oil and bake for 10 minutes.

7. Dish out in a platter and serve warm.

Nutrition value per serving

Calories: 387, Fat: 6g, Saturated Fat: 9.9g, Carbohydrates: 41g, Fiber: 2.9g, Sodium: 154mg, Protein: 6.6g

Energetic Bagel Platter

Prepping time: 5-10 minutes/ Cooking time:8 minutes /For 4 servings

Ingredients

- 4 bagels, halved
- 2 tablespoons coconut flakes
- 1 cup fine sugar
- 2 tablespoons black coffee, prepared and cooled down
- ¼ cup of coconut milk

Directions

1. Take your Ninja Foodi Grill and open the lid
2. Arrange grill grate and close top
3. Pre-heat Ninja Foodi by pressing the "GRILL" option and setting it to "MEDIUM."
4. Set the timer to 8 minutes
5. Let it pre-heat until you hear a beep
6. Arrange bagels over grill grate and lock lid
7. Cook for 2 minutes
8. Flip sausages and cook for 2 minutes more
9. Repeat the same procedure to Grill remaining Bagels
10. Take a mixing bowl and mix the remaining ingredients

11. Pour the sauce over grilled bagels
12. Serve and enjoy!

Nutrition value per serving

Calories: 300, Fat: 23 g, Saturated Fat: 12 g, Carbohydrates: 42 g, Fiber: 4 g, Sodium: 340 mg, Protein: 18 g

Classic French Burrito

Prepping time: 5-10 minutes/ Cooking time: 5 minutes /For 2 servings

Ingredients

- 2 tortillas
- ½ cup bacon, cooked crisp and crumbled
- ½ cup cheddar cheese, shredded
- 2 whole eggs, scrambled

Directions

1. Take a bowl and add eggs, bacon, and cheese
2. Top tortillas with the mix
3. Roll the tortillas, transfer to the Ninja Foodi Smart XL
4. Select AIR CRISP and cook for 5 minutes at 250 degrees F
5. Serve and enjoy!

Nutrition value per serving

Calories: 531, Fat: 15 g, Saturated Fat: 3 g, Carbohydrates: 81 g, Fiber: 2 g, Sodium: 1125 mg, Protein: 18 g

Sweet BBQ Chicken Meal

Prepping time: 5-10 minutes/ Cooking time: 40 minutes /For 4 servings

Ingredients

- Salt and pepper to taste
- 1 cup white vinegar

- ¾ cup onion, chopped
- ¼ cup tomato paste
- ¼ cup garlic, minced
- 1 cup of water
- 1 cup of soy sauce
- ¾ cup of sugar
- 6 chicken drumsticks

Directions

1. Take a Ziploc bag and add all ingredients to it
2. Marinate for at least 2 hours in your refrigerator
3. Insert the crisper basket, and close the hood
4. Preheat Ninja Foodi Smart XL by pressing the "AIR CRISP" option at 390 degrees F for 40 minutes
5. Place the grill pan accessory in the air fryer
6. Flip the chicken after every 10 minutes
7. Take a saucepan and pour the marinade into it, and heat over medium flame until sauce thickens
8. Brush with the glaze
9. Serve warm and enjoy!

Nutrition value per serving

Calories: 460, Fat: 20 g, Saturated Fat: 5 g, Carbohydrates: 26 g, Fiber: 3 g, Sodium: 126 mg, Protein: 28 g

Chapter 3: Chicken and Poultry Recipes

Easy Turkey Cutlets

Cooking time: 35 minutes /For 4 servings

Ingredients

- 1 egg
- 1 1/2 lbs turkey cutlets
- 1/2 cup breadcrumbs
- 1/2 tsp garlic powder
- 1/2 tsp onion powder
- 1/4 cup parmesan cheese, grated
- 1/4 tsp pepper
- 1/2 tsp salt

Directions

1. Season turkey cutlets with pepper and salt.
2. In a small bowl, add egg and whisk well.
3. In a shallow dish, mix breadcrumbs, garlic powder, cheese, and onion powder.
4. Dip each cutlet in egg then coat with breadcrumb mixture.
5. Place the cooking pot in the unit then close the hood.
6. Select bake mode then set the temperature to 350 F and set the timer to 25 minutes. Press start to begin preheating.
7. Once the unit is preheated it will beep then place coated turkey cutlets in the cooking pot. Close the hood.
8. Cook turkey cutlets for 25 minutes.
9. Serve and enjoy.

Nutrition value per serving

Calories 395; Fat 12 g; Carbohydrates 10.4 g; Sugar 1.1 g; Protein 56 g; Cholesterol 177 mg

Greek Chicken Breasts

Cooking time: 22 minutes /For 4 servings

Ingredients

- 4 chicken breasts
- 1 ½ tsp dried oregano
- 1 tsp paprika
- 6 garlic cloves, minced
- 6 tbsp fresh parsley, minced
- 6 tbsp olive oil
- 6 tbsp fresh lemon juice
- Pepper
- Salt

Directions

1. Add all ingredients except chicken into the zip-lock bag and mix well. Add chicken into the bag, seal bag shake well, and place in the refrigerator for overnight.

2. Place the cooking pot in the unit then place the grill grate in the pot and close the hood.

3. Select grill mode then set the temperature to medium and set the timer to 12 minutes. Press start to begin preheating.

4. Once the unit is preheated it will beep then place marinated chicken on grill grates and close the hood.

5. Cook chicken for 12 minutes or until the internal temperature of chicken reaches to 165 F.

6. Serve and enjoy.

Nutrition value per serving

Calories 475; Fat 32.2 g; Carbohydrates 3 g; Sugar 0.7 g; Protein 43 g; Cholesterol 130 mg

Meatballs

Cooking time: 35 minutes /For 6 servings

Ingredients

- 2 eggs, lightly beaten
- 2 lbs ground chicken
- 1 onion, diced
- 2 cups breadcrumbs
- 1/2 cup milk
- 1 tsp dry parsley
- 4 garlic cloves, minced
- Pepper
- Salt

Directions

- Add all ingredients into the mixing bowl and mix until well combined.
- Make balls from the meat mixture.
- Place the cooking pot in the unit then close the hood.
- Select bake mode then set the temperature to 390 F and set the timer to 25 minutes. Press start to begin preheating.
- Once the unit is preheated it will beep then place meatballs in the pot. Close the hood.
- Cook chicken meatballs for 25 minutes.
- Serve and enjoy.

Nutrition value per serving

Calories 470; Fat 15 g; Carbohydrates 29 g; Sugar 4 g; Protein 50 g; Cholesterol 190 mg

Simple Parmesan Chicken Breast

Cooking time: 25 minutes /For 4 servings

Ingredients

- 2 chicken breasts split in half
- 1 cup parmesan cheese, shredded
- 1 cup mayonnaise
- 1 cup breadcrumbs
- 1/4 tsp garlic powder
- Pepper
- Salt

Directions

1. In a shallow dish, mix parmesan cheese, breadcrumbs, garlic powder, pepper, and salt.

2. Spread mayonnaise on both sides of chicken breasts and coat chicken breasts with cheese mixture.

3. Place the cooking pot in the unit then place the crisper basket in the pot and close the hood.

4. Select air crisp mode then set the temperature to 390 F and set the timer to 15 minutes. Press start to begin preheating.

5. Once the unit is preheated it will beep then place coated chicken in the basket. Close the hood.

6. Cook chicken for 15 minutes.

7. Serve and enjoy.

Nutrition value per serving

Calories 545; Fat 30 g; Carbohydrates 34.3 g; Sugar 5.4 g; Protein 32.5 g; Cholesterol 96 mg

Italian Parmesan Chicken Breast

Cooking time: 24 minutes /For 4 servings

Ingredients

- 2 eggs, lightly beaten
- 1 lb chicken breast, skinless & boneless
- 1/2 tsp garlic powder
- 1 tsp Italian seasoning
- 1 cup parmesan cheese, grated
- 1/2 cup almond flour
- Pepper
- Salt

Directions

1. In a shallow bowl, add eggs and whisk well.
2. In a separate shallow dish, mix parmesan cheese, Italian seasoning, almond flour, garlic powder, pepper, and salt.
3. Dip chicken breast into the egg mixture and coat with cheese mixture.
4. Place the cooking pot in the unit then place the crisper basket in the pot and close the hood.
5. Select air crisp mode then set the temperature to 360 F and set the timer to 14 minutes. Press start to begin preheating.
6. Once the unit is preheated it will beep then place coated chicken in the basket. Close the hood.
7. Cook chicken for 7 minutes then flip chicken and continue cooking for 7 minutes.
8. Serve and enjoy.

Nutrition value per serving

Calories 375; Fat 19.7 g; Carbohydrates 3.4 g; Sugar 0.5 g; Protein 46.5 g; Cholesterol 195 mg

Crispy Chicken Breast

Cooking time: 45 minutes / For 4 servings

Ingredients

- 4 chicken breasts, skinless and boneless
- 2 eggs, lightly beaten
- 1/2 cup butter, cut into pieces
- 1 cup cracker crumbs
- Pepper
- Salt

Directions

- Add cracker crumbs and eggs in 2 separate shallow dishes.
- Mix cracker crumbs with pepper and salt.
- Dip chicken in the eggs and then coat with cracker crumb.
- Place the cooking pot in the unit then close the hood.
- Select bake mode then set the temperature to 375 F and set the timer to 35 minutes. Press start to begin preheating.
- Once the unit is preheated it will beep then arrange coated chicken into the cooking pot.
- Spread butter pieces on top of the chicken. Close the hood.
- Cook chicken for 30-35 minutes.
- Serve and enjoy.

Nutrition value per serving

Calories 590; Fat 40 g; Carbohydrates 9.7 g; Sugar 0.5 g; Protein 45 g; Cholesterol 273 mg

Flovrful Chicken Drumsticks

Cooking time: 55 minutes /For 4 servings

Ingredients

- 6 chicken legs
- 1/2 tsp oregano
- 1 1/2 tsp onion powder
- 1 tsp garlic powder
- 1/4 cup soy sauce
- 2 tbsp olive oil
- 1/2 tsp paprika
- 1/2 tsp pepper
- 1/2 tsp salt

Directions

1. Add chicken legs and remaining ingredients into the zip-lock bag, seal bag shake well and place in the refrigerator for 1 hour.

2. Place the cooking pot in the unit then close the hood.

3. Select bake mode then set the temperature to 375 F and set the timer to 45 minutes. Press start to begin preheating.

4. Once the unit is preheated it will beep then place marinated chicken legs in the cooking pot. Close the hood.

5. Cook chicken legs for 45 minutes.

6. Serve and enjoy.

Nutrition value per serving

Calories 315; Fat 20 g; Carbohydrates 2 g; Sugar 0.5 g; Protein 30.5 g; Cholesterol 105 mg

Sweet & Spicy Chicken

Cooking time: 22 minutes / For 4 servings

Ingredients

- 4 chicken thighs, skinless
- 2 tsp lemongrass, minced
- ½ tsp ginger, minced
- 1 tsp fish sauce
- 1 tsp soy sauce
- 1/3 cup sweet chili sauce
- Pepper
- Salt

Directions

1. Add all ingredients except chicken into the zip-lock bag and mix well. Add chicken into the bag, seal bag shake well, and place in the refrigerator for overnight.

2. Place the cooking pot in the unit then place the grill grate in the pot and close the hood.

3. Select grill mode then set the temperature to medium and set the timer to 12 minutes. Press start to begin preheating.

4. Once the unit is preheated it will beep then place marinated chicken thighs on grill grates and close the hood.

5. Cook chicken for 6 minutes then flip chicken and continue cooking for 6 minutes.

6. Serve and enjoy.

Nutrition value per serving

Calories 320; Fat 10.8 g; Carbohydrates 8.5 g; Sugar 8.1 g; Protein 42.4 g; Cholesterol 130 mg

Simple Baked Chicken Breasts

Cooking time: 30 minutes /For 6 servings

Ingredients

- 6 chicken breasts, skinless & boneless
- 1 tsp Italian seasoning
- 2 tbsp olive oil
- 1/4 tsp pepper
- 1/4 tsp paprika
- 1/2 tsp seasoning salt

Directions

1. Brush chicken with oil and season with paprika, Italian seasoning, pepper, and salt.
2. Place the cooking pot in the unit then close the hood.
3. Select bake mode then set the temperature to 400 F and set the timer to 20 minutes. Press start to begin preheating.
4. Once the unit is preheated it will beep then place chicken in the pot. Close the hood.
5. Cook chicken for 20 minutes.
6. Serve and enjoy.

Nutrition value per serving

Calories 320; Fat 15 g; Carbohydrates 0.2 g; Sugar 0.1 g; Protein 40 g; Cholesterol 130 mg

Easy Chicken Fajita

Cooking time: 26 minutes / For 4 servings

Ingredients

- 1 lb chicken breast, boneless, skinless & sliced
- 2 tsp olive oil
- 1 onion, sliced
- 2 bell peppers, sliced
- 1/8 tsp cayenne
- 1 tsp cumin
- 2 tsp chili powder
- Pepper
- Salt

Directions

- Add chicken, onion, and sliced bell peppers into the mixing bowl.
- Add cayenne, cumin, chili powder, oil, pepper, and salt and toss well.
- Place the cooking pot in the unit then place the crisper basket in the pot and close the hood.
- Select air crisp mode then set the temperature to 360 F and set the timer to 16 minutes. Press start to begin preheating.
- Once the unit is preheated it will beep then place chicken mixture into the basket. Close the hood.
- Cook chicken mixture for 8 minutes then stir and continue cooking for 8 minutes.
- Serve and enjoy.

Nutrition value per serving

Calories 185; Fat 5.7 g; Carbohydrates 8.1 g; Sugar 4.3 g; Protein 25.2 g; Cholesterol 75 mg

Tasty Parmesan Chicken Wings

Cooking time: 35 minutes /For 4 servings

Ingredients

- 1 1/2 lbs chicken wings
- 1/4 cup parmesan cheese, grated
- 2 tbsp flour
- 3/4 tbsp garlic powder
- Pepper
- Salt

Directions

1. In a large bowl, mix garlic powder, parmesan cheese, flour, pepper, and salt. Add chicken wings and toss until well coated.
2. Place the cooking pot in the unit then place the crisper basket in the pot and close the hood.
3. Select air crisp mode then set the temperature to 380 F and set the timer to 25 minutes. Press start to begin preheating.
4. Once the unit is preheated it will beep then place chicken wings in the basket. Close the hood.
5. Cook chicken wings for 25 minutes. Flip chicken wings halfway through.
6. Serve and enjoy.

Nutrition value per serving

Calories 385; Fat 15 g; Carbohydrates 5.6 g; Sugar 0.4 g; Protein 53.5 g; Cholesterol 160 mg

Lemon Pepper Chicken

Cooking time: 30 minutes /For 6 servings

Ingredients

- 6 chicken breast, boneless
- 2 lemon juice
- ½ onion, diced
- 2 tsp garlic, minced
- ½ cup olive oil
- 1 tsp pepper
- 1 tsp salt

Directions

1. Add all ingredients except chicken into the zip-lock bag and mix well. Add chicken into the bag, seal bag shake well, and place in the refrigerator for overnight.

2. Place the cooking pot in the unit then place the grill grate in the pot and close the hood.

3. Select grill mode then set the temperature to medium and set the timer to 20 minutes. Press start to begin preheating.

4. Once the unit is preheated it will beep then place marinated chicken on grill grates and close the hood.

5. Cook chicken for 20 minutes. Flip chicken after every 5 minutes.

6. Serve and enjoy.

Nutrition value per serving

Calories 431; Fat 27.8 g; Carbohydrates 1.7 g; Sugar 0.7 g; Protein 42.6 g; Cholesterol 130 mg

Flavorful & Juicy Grilled Chicken

Cooking time: 22 minutes /For 4 servings

Ingredients

- 4 chicken breasts
- ½ tsp ground coriander
- 2 tbsp olive oil
- ½ tsp smoked paprika
- 1 tsp ground cumin
- 1 tsp garlic powder
- ¼ tsp pepper
- ½ tsp sea salt

Directions

1. Place the cooking pot in the unit then place the grill grate in the pot and close the hood.

2. Select grill mode then set the temperature to medium and set the timer to 12 minutes. Press start to begin preheating.

3. In a small bowl, mix oil, paprika, coriander, cumin, garlic powder, pepper, and salt and rub all over the chicken breasts.

4. Once the unit is preheated it will beep then place chicken breasts on grill grates and close the hood.

5. Cook chicken for 6 minutes then flip chicken and continue cooking for 6 minutes.

6. Serve and enjoy.

Nutrition value per serving

Calories 343; Fat 18 g; Carbohydrates 1 g; Sugar 0.2 g; Protein 42.5 g; Cholesterol 130 mg

Meatballs

Cooking time: 15 minutes / For 6 servings

Ingredients

- 2 eggs
- 2 lbs ground chicken
- 1/2 cup ricotta cheese
- 1/4 cup fresh parsley, chopped
- 1/2 cup almond flour
- 1 tsp pepper
- 2 tsp salt

Directions

1. Add all ingredients into the large mixing bowl and mix until well combined.
2. Make small balls from the meat mixture.
3. Place the cooking pot in the unit then place the crisper basket in the pot and close the hood.
4. Select air crisp mode then set the temperature to 380 F and set the timer to 10 minutes. Press start to begin preheating.
5. Once the unit is preheated it will beep then place meatballs in the basket. Close the hood.
6. Cook meatballs for 10 minutes.
7. Serve and enjoy.

Nutrition value per serving

Calories 225; Fat 5.6 g; Carbohydrates 2.1 g; Sugar 0.3 g; Protein 43 g; Cholesterol 155 mg

Crispy Chicken Wings

Cooking time: 30 minutes / For 4 servings

Ingredients

- 1 lb chicken wings
- ½ tbsp black peppercorns, crushed
- 1 tbsp olive oil
- ¼ tsp brown sugar
- ¼ tbsp ground coriander
- ¼ tbsp ground cumin
- ¼ tsp five-spice powder
- 1 tsp baking powder
- ¼ tsp garlic powder
- 1 tsp kosher salt

Directions

1. Add all ingredients except chicken wings into the zip-lock bag and mix well. Add chicken wings into the bag, seal bag shake well, and place in the refrigerator for overnight.

2. Place the cooking pot in the unit then place the grill grate in the pot and close the hood.

3. Select grill mode then set the temperature to medium and set the timer to 20 minutes. Press start to begin preheating.

4. Once the unit is preheated it will beep then place marinated chicken wings on grill grates and close the hood.

5. Cook chicken wings for 20 minutes. Flip chicken wings after every 5 minutes and cook for 20 minutes or until the internal temperature of chicken wings reaches to 165 F.

6. Serve and enjoy.

Nutrition value per serving

Calories 72; Fat 4 g; Carbohydrates 8 g; Sugar 3 g; Protein 2 g; Cholesterol 0 mg

Chapter 4: Meat Recipes

Spicy Baked Pork Chops

Cooking time: 20 minutes / For 4 servings

Ingredients

- 4 pork chops
- 1/2 tsp dried sage
- 1 tsp cayenne pepper
- 1 tsp paprika
- 1/2 tsp black pepper
- 1/2 tsp ground cumin
- 1 1/2 tsp olive oil
- 1/2 tsp garlic salt

Directions

1. Place the cooking pot in the unit then close the hood.
2. Select bake mode then set the temperature to 400 F and set the timer to 10 minutes. Press start to begin preheating.
3. In a small bowl, mix paprika, garlic salt, sage, pepper, cayenne pepper, and cumin.
4. Rub pork chops with spice mixture.
5. Once the unit is preheated it will beep then place pork chops in the cooking pot. Close the hood.
6. Cook pork chops for 10 minutes.
7. Serve and enjoy.

Nutrition value per serving

Calories 275; Fat 22 g; Carbohydrates 1.1 g; Sugar 0.2 g; Protein 18.3 g; Cholesterol 69 mg

Rosemary Lamb Chops

Cooking time: 20 minutes /For 4 servings

Ingredients

- 8 lamb loin chops
- 1 tbsp fresh rosemary, chopped
- ¼ cup fresh lemon juice
- 6 garlic cloves, crushed
- 1 tsp olive oil
- ¼ tsp black pepper
- 1 ¼ tsp kosher salt

Directions

1. Add all ingredients except pork chops into the zip-lock bag and mix well. Add pork chops into the bag, seal bag shake well, and place in the refrigerator for overnight.
2. Place the cooking pot in the unit then place the grill grate in the pot and close the hood.
3. Select grill mode then set the temperature to medium and set the timer to 10 minutes. Press start to begin preheating.
4. Once the unit is preheated it will beep then place marinated pork chops on grill grates and close the hood.
5. Cook pork chops for 5 minutes then flip pork chops and continue cooking for 5 minutes.
6. Serve and enjoy.

Nutrition value per serving

Calories 389; Fat 17.4 g; Carbohydrates 2.4 g; Sugar 0.4 g; Protein 50.5 g; Cholesterol 160 mg

Baked Lamb Patties

Cooking time: 25 minutes / For 4 servings

Ingredients

- 1 lb ground lamb
- 1 tsp ground cinnamon
- 1 tbsp garlic, chopped
- 1/2 tsp ground allspice
- 1 tsp ground cumin
- 1/4 tsp cayenne pepper
- 1/4 cup fresh parsley, chopped
- 1/4 cup onion, minced
- 1/4 tsp pepper
- 1 tsp ground coriander
- 1 tsp kosher salt

Directions

- Place the cooking pot in the unit then close the hood.
- Select bake mode then set the temperature to 375 F and set the timer to 15 minutes. Press start to begin preheating.
- Add all ingredients into the large bowl and mix until well combined.
- Make patties from the meat mixture.
- Once the unit is preheated it will beep then place patties in the cooking pot. Close the hood.
- Bake patties for 15 minutes. Turn patties halfway through.
- Serve and enjoy.

Nutrition value per serving

Calories 225; Fat 8 g; Carbohydrates 2.6 g; Sugar 0.4 g; Protein 32 g; Cholesterol 102 mg

Garlic Butter Steak

Cooking time: 22 minutes /For 4 servings

Ingredients

- 2 rib-eye steak
- 2 tsp garlic, minced
- 2 tbsp fresh parsley, chopped
- 1 stick butter, softened
- 1 tsp Worcestershire sauce
- Pepper
- Salt

Directions

1. Place the cooking pot in the unit then place the crisper basket in the pot and close the hood.
2. Select air crisp mode then set the temperature to 400 F and set the timer to 12 minutes. Press start to begin preheating.
3. In a bowl, mix butter, Worcestershire sauce, garlic, parsley, and salt and place in the refrigerator.
4. Season steak with pepper and salt.
5. Once the unit is preheated it will beep then place seasoned steak in the basket. Close the hood.
6. Cook steak for 12 minutes.
7. Remove steak from the basket and top with butter mixture.
8. Serve and enjoy.

Nutrition value per serving

Calories 592; Fat 58 g; Carbohydrates 2.9 g; Sugar 0.6 g; Protein 16 g; Cholesterol 121 mg

Air Fry Sausage Balls

Cooking time: 25 minutes / For 4 servings

Ingredients

- 4 oz sausage meat
- 3 tbsp almond flour
- 1 tsp sage
- 1/2 tsp ginger garlic paste
- 1/2 onion, diced
- Pepper
- Salt

Directions

1. Place the cooking pot in the unit then place the crisper basket in the pot and close the hood.

2. Select air crisp mode then set the temperature to 360 F and set the timer to 15 minutes. Press start to begin preheating.

3. Add all ingredients into the mixing bowl and mix until well combined.

4. Make balls from the meat mixture.

5. Once the unit is preheated it will beep then place meatballs in the basket. Close the hood.

6. Cook meatballs for 15 minutes.

7. Serve and enjoy.

Nutrition value per serving

Calories 135; Fat 10 g; Carbohydrates 2.7 g; Sugar 0.6 g; Protein 6.8 g; Cholesterol 24 mg

Asian Short Ribs

Cooking time: 20 minutes /For 4 servings

Ingredients

- 1 lb flanken cut short ribs
- For marinade:
- 1/4-inch ginger piece, peeled
- 5 garlic cloves
- ½ pear, peeled & cored
- ½ medium onion
- 1 tbsp sesame oil
- ½ cup sugar
- ½ cup soy sauce
- ½ tbsp ground black pepper

Directions

1. Add all marinade ingredients into the blender and blend until well combined.
2. Add ribs into the zip-lock bag then pour marinade over ribs, seal bag shake well, and place in the refrigerator for overnight.
3. Place the cooking pot in the unit then place the grill grate in the pot and close the hood.
4. Select grill mode then set the temperature to high and set the timer to 10 minutes. Press start to begin preheating.
5. Once the unit is preheated it will beep then place marinated ribs on grill grates and close the hood.
6. Cook ribs for 5 minutes then flip ribs and continue cooking for 5 minutes.
7. Serve and enjoy.

Nutrition value per serving

Calories 475; Fat 29.6 g; Carbohydrates 33.1 g; Sugar 27.9 g; Protein 21.6 g; Cholesterol 75 mg

Air Fry Sirloin Steak

Cooking time: 20 minutes /For 4 servings

Ingredients

- 2 sirloin steaks
- 2 tbsp steak seasoning
- 2 tsp olive oil

Directions

1. Place the cooking pot in the unit then place the crisper basket in the pot and close the hood.

2. Select air crisp mode then set the temperature to 350 F and set the timer to 10 minutes. Press start to begin preheating.

3. Brush steak with olive oil and season with steak seasoning.

4. Once the unit is preheated it will beep then place steak in the basket. Close the hood.

5. Cook steak for 10 minutes.

6. Slice and serve.

Nutrition value per serving

Calories 195; Fat 10 g; Carbohydrates 0 g; Sugar 0 g; Protein 25 g; Cholesterol 76 mg

Meatballs

Cooking time: 30 minutes /For 4 servings

Ingredients

- 1 lb ground beef
- 2 tbsp fresh parsley, chopped
- 1/2 cup almond flour
- 1/4 cup onion, chopped
- 3 tbsp mushrooms, chopped
- 1/4 tsp pepper
- 1 tsp salt

Directions

1. Place the cooking pot in the unit then place the crisper basket in the pot and close the hood.
2. Select air crisp mode then set the temperature to 350 F and set the timer to 20 minutes. Press start to begin preheating.
3. In a bowl, mix together ground beef, parsley, onions, and mushrooms.
4. Add remaining ingredients and mix until well combined.
5. Make balls from the mixture.
6. Once the unit is preheated it will beep then place meatballs in the basket. Close the hood.
7. Cook meatballs for 20 minutes.
8. Serve and enjoy.

Nutrition value per serving

Calories 101; Fat 4 g; Carbohydrates 1.3 g; Sugar 0.1 g; Protein 12 g; Cholesterol 34 mg

Meatballs

Cooking time: 30 minutes /For 4 servings

Ingredients

- 1/2 lb ground beef
- 1/2 tsp garlic powder
- 1/2 tsp onion powder
- 1/2 lb Italian sausage
- 1/2 cup cheddar cheese, shredded
- Pepper
- Salt

Directions

1. Place the cooking pot in the unit then place the crisper basket in the pot and close the hood.

2. Select air crisp mode then set the temperature to 370 F and set the timer to 20 minutes. Press start to begin preheating.

3. Add all ingredients into the large bowl and mix until well combined.

4. Make balls from the mixture.

5. Once the unit is preheated it will beep then place meatballs in the basket. Close the hood.

6. Cook meatballs for 20 minutes.

7. Serve and enjoy.

Nutrition value per serving

Calories 355; Fat 24 g; Carbohydrates 0.8 g; Sugar 0.3 g; Protein 32 g; Cholesterol 113 mg

Easy Montreal Seasoned Steak

Cooking time: 17 minutes /For 2 servings

Ingredients

- 12 oz steaks
- 1 tbsp soy sauce
- 1/2 tbsp cocoa powder
- 1 tbsp Montreal steak seasoning
- Pepper
- Salt

Directions

1. Place the cooking pot in the unit then place the crisper basket in the pot and close the hood.
2. Select air crisp mode then set the temperature to 375 F and set the timer to 7 minutes. Press start to begin preheating.
3. Add steak, liquid smoke, soy sauce, and steak seasonings into the large zip-lock bag. Seal bag and place it in the refrigerator overnight.
4. Once the unit is preheated it will beep then place marinated steaks in the basket. Close the hood.
5. Cook steaks for 7 minutes.
6. Serve and enjoy.

Nutrition value per serving

Calories 355; Fat 8.7 g; Carbohydrates 1.4 g; Sugar 0.2 g; Protein 62 g; Cholesterol 153 mg

Easy Burger Patty

Cooking time: 30 minutes /For 4 servings

Ingredients

- 1 lb ground beef
- 1 tbsp steak sauce
- 1 tsp garlic, minced
- Pepper
- Salt

Directions

1. Add all ingredients into the mixing bowl and mix until well combined.
2. Make four equal shapes of patties from the mixture.
3. Place the cooking pot in the unit then place the grill grate in the pot and close the hood.
4. Select grill mode then set the temperature to medium and set the timer to 20 minutes. Press start to begin preheating.
5. Once the unit is preheated it will beep then place patties on grill grates and close the hood.
6. Cook patties for 10 minutes then flip patties and continue cooking for 10 minutes.
7. Serve and enjoy.

Nutrition value per serving

Calories 212; Fat 7.1 g; Carbohydrates 0.3 g; Sugar 0 g; Protein 34.4 g; Cholesterol 101 mg

Sweet & Savory Pork Chops

Cooking time: 22 minutes / For 4 servings

Ingredients

- 4 pork loin chops
- For rub:
- ½ tsp cayenne pepper
- ½ tsp ground mustard
- 1 tsp paprika
- 2 tbsp brown sugar
- 1 tsp black pepper
- 2 tsp kosher salt

Directions

1. In a small bowl mix rub ingredients and rub all over pork chops.

2. Place the cooking pot in the unit then place the grill grate in the pot and close the hood.

3. Select grill mode then set the temperature to high and set the timer to 12 minutes. Press start to begin preheating.

4. Once the unit is preheated it will beep then place pork chops on grill grates and close the hood.

5. Cook pork chops for 6 minutes then flip pork chops and continue cooking for 6 minutes or until internal temperature reaches to 145 F.

6. Serve and enjoy.

Nutrition value per serving

Calories 279; Fat 20.1 g; Carbohydrates 5.3 g; Sugar 4.5 g; Protein 18.3 g; Cholesterol 69 mg

Marinated Pork Chops

Cooking time: 24 minutes / For 2 servings

Ingredients

- 2 pork chops
- For marinade:
- 1 tbsp brown sugar
- ¼ cup soy sauce
- ¼ cup fresh lemon juice
- 1/3 cup olive oil
- ½ tsp oregano
- 1 tsp onion powder
- Pepper
- Salt

Directions

1. Add all marinade ingredients into the zip-lock bag and mix well.
2. Add pork chops into the zip-lock bag, seal bag shake well and place in the refrigerator for overnight.
3. Place the cooking pot in the unit then place the grill grate in the pot and close the hood.
4. Select grill mode then set the temperature to medium and set the timer to 14 minutes. Press start to begin preheating.
5. Once the unit is preheated it will beep then place marinated pork chops on grill grates and close the hood.
6. Cook pork chops for 7 minutes then flip pork chops and continue cooking for 7 minutes.
7. Serve and enjoy.

Nutrition value per serving

Calories 591; Fat 53.8 g; Carbohydrates 8.7 g; Sugar 6 g; Protein 20.4 g; Cholesterol 69 mg

Delicious Beef Patties

Cooking time: 30 minutes /For 4 servings

Ingredients

- 10 oz ground beef
- 1 tsp tomato puree
- 1 tsp garlic puree
- 1 oz cheddar cheese
- 1 tsp basil
- 1 tsp mustard
- 1 tsp mixed herbs
- Pepper
- Salt

Directions

1. Place the cooking pot in the unit then place the crisper basket in the pot and close the hood.
2. Select air crisp mode then set the temperature to 350 F and set the timer to 20 minutes. Press start to begin preheating.
3. Add all ingredients into the large bowl and mix until well combined.
4. Make four patties from the mixture.
5. Once the unit is preheated it will beep then place patties in the basket. Close the hood.
6. Cook patties for 20 minutes.
7. Serve and enjoy.

Nutrition value per serving

Calories 165; Fat 7.3 g; Carbohydrates 0.6 g; Sugar 0.2 g; Protein 24 g; Cholesterol 71 mg

Flavorful Marinated Steak

Cooking time: 22 minutes /For 4 servings

Ingredients

- 4 ribeye steaks
- 1 tsp ground white pepper
- 3 tbsp dried basil
- 1 ½ tbsp garlic powder
- ¼ cup Worcestershire sauce
- 1 lemon juice
- ½ cup olive oil
- 1/3 cup soy sauce

Directions

1. Add all ingredients except steaks into the zip-lock bag and mix well. Add steaks into the bag, seal bag shake well, and place in the refrigerator for overnight.

2. Place the cooking pot in the unit then place the grill grate in the pot and close the hood.

3. Select grill mode then set the temperature to high and set the timer to 12 minutes. Press start to begin preheating.

4. Once the unit is preheated it will beep then place marinated steaks on grill grates and close the hood.

5. Cook steaks for 6 minutes then flip steaks and continue cooking for 6 minutes.

6. Serve and enjoy.

Nutrition value per serving

Calories 892; Fat 69.4 g; Carbohydrates 7.6 g; Sugar 4.4 g; Protein 2.1 g; Cholesterol 0 mg

Chapter 5: Snacks Recipes

Basil Pizzas

Prepping time: 10 minutes/ Cooking time: 17 minutes / For 4 servings

Ingredients

- 4(4 ounces) Italian sausage, sliced
- 4 flatbreads
- 1/4 cup olive oil
- 2 cups mozzarella cheese, shredded
- 1/2 cup fresh basil, thinly sliced
- 1 cup tomato basil pasta sauce
- 1/2 cup parmesan cheese, grated

Directions

1. Pre-heat Ninja Foodi by pressing the "GRILL" option and setting it to "HIGH"
2. Once preheated, open the lid and place the sliced sausage on the grill
3. Cover the lid and grill for 3 minutes per side
4. Take all the ingredients for burger except oil and the bun in a bowl
5. Mix them and then make 4 of the ½ inch patties out of it
6. Brush these patties with olive oil
7. Pre-heat Ninja Foodi by pressing the "GRILL" option and setting it to "HIGH"
8. Once it pre-heat until you hear a beep, open the lid
9. Place 2 patties in the grill grate and cook for 5 minutes
10. Grill the remaining patties in the same way
11. Serve and enjoy!

Nutrition value per serving

Calories: 308 kcal, Carbs: 30 g, Fat: 20.5 g. Protein: 49 g

Seared Tuna Salad

Prepping time: 10 minutes/ Cooking time: 6 minutes/ For 4 servings

Ingredients

- 1 and 1/2 pounds ahi tuna, cut into four strips
- 2 tablespoons sesame oil
- 1(10 ounces) bag baby greens
- 2 tablespoons of rice wine vinegar
- 6 tablespoons extra-virgin olive oil
- 1/2 English cucumber, sliced
- 1/4 teaspoon of sea salt
- 1/2 teaspoon black pepper, freshly ground

Directions

1. Insert the grill grate and close the hood
2. Pre-heat Ninja Foodi by pressing the "GRILL" option at and setting it to "MAX" and timer to 6 minutes
3. Take a small bowl, whisk together the rice vinegar, salt, and pepper
4. Slowly pour in the oil while whisking until vinaigrette is fully combined
5. Season the tuna with salt and pepper, drizzle with the sesame oil
6. Once it pre-heat until you hear a beep
7. Arrange the shrimp over the grill grate, lock lid and cook for 6 minutes
8. Do not flip during cooking
9. Once cooked completely, top salad with tuna strip
10. Drizzle the vinaigrette over the top
11. Serve immediately and enjoy!

Nutrition value per serving

Calories: 427 kcal, Carbs: 5 g, Fat: 30 g. Protein: 36 g

Fajita Skewers

Prepping time: 10 minutes/ Cooking time: 14 minutes / For 8 servings

Ingredients

- 1 pound sirloin steak, cubed
- Olive oil, for drizzling
- 1 bunch scallions, cut into large pieces
- 4 large bell pepper, cubed
- 1 pack tortillas, torn
- Salt to taste
- Black pepper, grounded

Directions

1. Thread the steak, tortillas, scallions, and pepper on the skewers
2. Drizzle olive oil, salt, black pepper over the skewers
3. Pre-heat Ninja Foodi by pressing the "GRILL" option and setting it to "MED"
4. Once preheated, open the lid and place 4 skewers on the grill
5. Cover the lid and grill for 7 minutes
6. Keep rotating skewers for every 2 minutes
7. Serve warm and enjoy!

Nutrition value per serving

Calories: 353 kcal, Carbs: 11 g, Fat: 7.5 g. Protein: 13.1 g

Lemon-Garlic Shrimp Caesar Salad

Prepping time: 10 minutes/ Cooking time: 5 minutes/ For 4 servings

Ingredients

- 1 pound fresh jumbo shrimp
- 2 heads romaine lettuce, chopped
- 3/4 cup Caesar dressing
- 1/2 cup parmesan cheese, grated
- 1/2 lemon juice
- 3 garlic cloves, minced
- Sea salt
- Black pepper, grounded

Directions

1. Insert the grill grate and close the hood

2. Pre-heat Ninja Foodi by pressing the "GRILL" option at and setting it to "MAX" and timer to 5 minutes

3. Take a large bowl, toss the shrimp with the lemon juice, garlic, salt, and pepper

4. Let it marinate while the grill is preheating

5. Once it pre-heat until you hear a beep

6. Arrange the shrimp over the grill grate, lock lid and cook for 5 minutes

7. Toss the romaine lettuce with the Caesar dressing

8. Once cooked completely, remove the shrimp from the grill

9. Sprinkle with parmesan cheese

10. Serve and enjoy!

Nutrition value per serving

Calories: 279 kcal, Carbs: 17 g, Fat: 11 g. Protein: 30 g

Crispy Rosemary Potatoes

Prepping time: 10 minutes/ Cooking time: 20 minutes/ For 4 servings

Ingredients

- 2 pounds baby red potatoes, quartered
- 2 tablespoons extra virgin olive oil
- 1/4 cup dried onion flakes
- 1/2 teaspoon onion powder
- 1/2 teaspoon garlic powder
- 1/4 teaspoon celery powder
- 1/4 teaspoon freshly ground black pepper
- 1/2 teaspoon dried parsley
- 1/2 teaspoon salt

Directions

1. Take a large bowl and add all listed ingredients, toss well and coat them well

2. Pre-heat Ninja Foodi by pressing the "AIR CRISP" option and setting it to "390 Degrees F" and timer to 20 minutes

3. let it pre-heat until you hear a beep

4. Once preheated, add potatoes to the cooking basket

5. Lock and cook for 10 minutes, making sure to shake the basket and cook for 10 minutes more

6. Once done, check the crispiness, if it's alright, serve away.

7. If not, cook for 5 minutes more

8. Enjoy!

Nutrition value per serving

Calories: 232 kcal, Carbs: 39 g, Fat: 7 g. Protein: 4 g

Honey Mustard Chicken Tenders

Prepping time: 5 minutes/ Cooking time: 3 minutes / For 4 servings

Ingredients

- 2 pounds chicken tenders
- 1/2 cup Dijon mustard
- 1/2 cup walnuts
- 2 tablespoons honey
- 2 tablespoons olive oil
- 1 teaspoon black pepper, ground

Directions

1. Take a medium bowl and whisk together the mustard, olive oil, honey, and pepper into it
2. Add the chicken and toss to coat
3. Grind the walnut in your food processor
4. Insert the grill grate and close the hood
5. Pre-heat Ninja Foodi by pressing the "GRILL" option and setting it to "HIGH" for 4 minutes
6. Toss the chicken tenders in the ground walnuts to coat them lightly
7. Grill the chicken tender for 3 minutes
8. Serve hot and enjoy!

Nutrition value per serving

Calories: 444 kcal, Carbs: 26 g, Fat: 20 g. Protein: 6 g

Portobello and Pesto Sliders

Prepping time: 10 minutes/ Cooking time: 8 minutes/ For 4 servings

Ingredients

- 8 small portobello mushrooms, trimmed with gills removed
- 1 tomato, sliced
- 2 tablespoons canola oil
- 1/2 cup pesto
- 1/2 cup microgreens
- 2 tablespoons balsamic vinegar
- 8 slider buns

Directions

1. Insert the grill grate and close the hood
2. Pre-heat Ninja Foodi by pressing the "GRILL" option at and setting it to "HIGH" and timer to 8 minutes
3. Brush the mushrooms with oil and balsamic vinegar
4. Once it pre-heat until you hear a beep
5. Arrange the mushrooms over the grill grate, lock lid and cook for 8 minutes
6. Once cooked, removed the mushrooms from the grill and layer on the buns with tomato, pesto, and microgreens
7. Serve immediately and enjoy!

Nutrition value per serving

Calories: 373 kcal, Carbs: 33 g, Fat: 22 g. Protein: 12 g

Bacon Brussels Delight

Prepping time: 5-10 minutes/ Cooking time: 12 minutes/ For 4 servings

Ingredients

- 6 slices bacon, chopped
- 1 pound Brussels sprouts, halved
- 1/2 teaspoon black pepper
- 1 tablespoon of sea salt
- 2 tablespoons olive oil, extra-virgin

Directions

1. Take a mixing bowl and toss the brussels sprouts, olive oil, bacon, salt, and black pepper

2. Arrange the crisping basket inside the pot

3. Pre-heat Ninja Foodi by pressing the "AIR CRISP" option at 390 degrees F and timer to 12 minutes

4. Let it pre-heat until you hear a beep

5. Arrange the brussels sprout mixture directly inside the basket

6. Close the top lid and cook for 6 minutes, then shake the basket

7. Close the top lid and cook for 6 minutes more

8. Serve warm and enjoy!

Nutrition value per serving

Calories: 279 kcal, Carbs: 12.5 g, Fat: 18.5 g. Protein: 14.5 g

Juicy Honey Carrots

Prepping time: 10 minutes/ Cooking time: 10 minutes/ For 4 servings

Ingredients

- 2 tablespoons melted butter
- 6 carrots, cut lengthwise
- 1 tablespoon parsley, chopped
- 1 tablespoon rosemary, chopped
- 1 tablespoon honey
- 1 teaspoon salt

Directions

1. Take your Ninja Foodi Smart XL Grill and open lid, arrange grill grate and close top
2. Pre-heat Ninja Foodi by pressing the "GRILL" option and setting it to "MAX" and timer to 10 minutes
3. let it pre-heat until you hear a beep
4. Arrange carrots over grill grate and spread the remaining ingredients and drizzle honey, lock lid and cook for 5 minutes, flip sausages and cook for 5 minutes more
5. Once done, serve and enjoy!

Nutrition value per serving

Calories: 80 kcal, Carbs: 10 g, Fat: 4 g. Protein: 0.5 g

Seasoned Broccoli Dish

Prepping time: 10 minutes/ Cooking time: 10 minutes/ For 4 servings

Ingredients

- 1 pound broccoli, cut into florets
- 1/4 teaspoon turmeric powder
- 1 tablespoon chickpea flour
- 2 tablespoons yogurt
- 1/4 teaspoon spice mix
- 1/2 teaspoon red chili powder
- 1/2 teaspoon salt

Directions

1. Wash the broccoli florets thoroughly
2. Take a mixing bowl and add all ingredients except florets, mix well
3. Add florets to the mix and let them sit in the fridge for 30 minutes
4. Take your Ninja Foodi Smart XL Grill and open lid, arrange grill grate and close top
5. Pre-heat Ninja Foodi by pressing the "AIR CRISP" option and setting it to "390 Degrees F and timer to 10 minutes
6. let it pre-heat until you hear a beep
7. Arrange florets over the Grill Basket and lock lid, cook for 10 minutes
8. Serve and enjoy!

Nutrition value per serving

Calories: 113 kcal, Carbs: 12 g, Fat: 2 g. Protein: 0.7 g

Spicy Barbecue Chicken Drumsticks_

Prepping time: 10 minutes/ Cooking time: 20 minutes/ For 4 servings

Ingredients

- 1 pound chicken drumsticks
- 2 cups barbecue sauce
- 1 tablespoon hot sauce
- 1 lime juice
- 2 tablespoons honey
- Sea salt
- Black pepper, freshly grounded

Directions

1. Take a large bowl and combine with barbecue sauce, honey, lime juice, and hot sauce
2. Season with salt and pepper, set aside ½ cup of the sauce
3. Add drumsticks to the bowl and toss until coat well
4. Insert the grill grate and close the hood
5. Pre-heat Ninja Foodi by pressing the "GRILL" option at and setting it to "MED" and timer to 20 minutes
6. Let it pre-heat until you hear a beep
7. Arrange the drumsticks over the grill grate, lock lid and cook for 18 minutes
8. Basting often during cooking
9. Cook until the temperature reaches 165 degrees F
10. Cook 2 minutes more if necessary
11. Serve and enjoy!

Nutrition value per serving

Calories: 433 kcal, Carbs: 55 g, Fat: 14 g. Protein: 21 g

Simple Crispy Brussels

Prepping time: 10 minutes/ Cooking time: 12 minutes/ For 4 servings

Ingredients

- 1 pound brussels sprouts, halved
- 2 tablespoons olive oil, extra virgin
- 1/2 teaspoon ground black pepper
- 1 teaspoon salt
- 6 slices bacon, chopped

Directions

1. Take a mixing bowl and add Brussels, olive oil, salt, pepper, and bacon

2. Pre-heat Ninja Foodi by pressing the "AIR CRISP" option and setting it to "390 degrees F" and timer to 12 minutes

3. Let it pre-heat until you hear a beep

4. Arrange Brussels over basket and lock lid, cook for 6 minutes, shake and cook for 6 minutes more

5. Serve and enjoy!

Nutrition value per serving

Calories: 279 kcal, Carbs: 12 g, Fat: 18 g. Protein: 14 g

Cajun Eggplant Appetizer

Prepping time: 5-10 minutes/ Cooking time: 10 minutes/ For 4 servings

Ingredients

- 2 small eggplants, cut into slices
- 1/4 cup olive oil
- 2 tablespoons lime juice
- 3 teaspoons cajun seasoning

Directions

1. Coat the eggplant slices with oil, lemon juices and cajun seasoning Add the chicken wings and combine well to coat

2. Arrange the grill grate and close the lid

3. Pre-heat Ninja Foodi by pressing the "GRILL" option and setting it to "MED" and timer to 10 minutes

4. Let it pre-heat until you hear a beep

5. Arrange the eggplant slices over the grill grate, lock lid and cook for 5 minutes

6. Flip the chicken and close the lid, cook for 5 minutes more

7. Serve warm and enjoy!

Nutrition value per serving

Calories: 362 kcal, Carbs: 16 g, Fat: 11 g. Protein: 8 g

Grilled Eggplant, Tomato and Mozzarella Stacks

Prepping time: 10 minutes/ Cooking time: 14 minutes/ For 4 servings

Ingredients

- 1 eggplant, sliced and 1/4 inch thick
- 2 beefsteak or heirloom tomatoes, sliced 1/4 inch thick
- 1/2 pound buffalo mozzarella, sliced 1/4 inch thick
- 2 tablespoons canola oil
- 12 large basil leaves
- Sea salt

Directions

1. Insert the grill grate and close the hood
2. Pre-heat Ninja Foodi by pressing the "GRILL" option at and setting it to "MAX" and timer to 14 minutes
3. Take a large bowl and toss the eggplant and oil until evenly coated
4. Once it pre-heat until you hear a beep
5. Arrange the eggplant over the grill grate, lock lid and cook for 8 to 12 minutes
6. After 8 to 12 minutes, top the eggplant with one slice each of the tomato and mozzarella
7. Close the hood and grill for 2 minutes
8. Once cooked, remove the eggplant stacks from the grill
9. Place 2 or 3 basil leaves on top of half
10. Season the remaining eggplant with salt, garnish with the remaining basil
11. Serve and enjoy!

Nutrition value per serving

Calories: 284 kcal, Carbs: 13 g, Fat: 20 g. Protein: 15 g

Honey Asparagus

Prepping time: 10 minutes/ Cooking time: 15 minutes/ For 4 servings

Ingredients

- 2 pounds asparagus, trimmed
- 1/2 teaspoon pepper
- 1 teaspoon salt
- 1/4 cup honey
- 2 tablespoons olive oil
- 4 tablespoons tarragon, minced

Directions

1. Take a bowl and add asparagus, oil, salt, honey, pepper, tarragon and toss well

2. Pre-heat Ninja Foodi by pressing the "GRILL" option and setting it to "MED" and timer to 8 minutes

3. Let it pre-heat until you hear a beep

4. Arrange asparagus over grill grate, lock lid and cook for 4 minutes, flip asparagus and cook for 4 minutes more

5. Serve and enjoy!

Nutrition value per serving

Calories: 240 kcal, Carbs: 31 g, Fat: 15 g. Protein: 7 g

Crispy Potato Cubes

Prepping time: 10 minutes/ Cooking time: 20 minutes/ For 4 servings

Ingredients

- 1 pound potato, peeled
- 1 tablespoon olive oil
- 1 teaspoon dried dill
- 1 teaspoon dried oregano
- 1/4 teaspoon chili flakes

Directions

1. Pre-heat Ninja Foodi by pressing the "AIR CRISP" option and setting it to "400 Degrees F" and timer to 20 minutes
2. let it pre-heat until you hear a beep
3. Cut potatoes into cubes
4. Sprinkle potato cubes with dill, oregano and chili flakes
5. Transfer to Foodi Grill and cook for 15 minutes
6. Stir while cooking, once they are crunchy
7. Serve and enjoy!

Nutrition value per serving

Calories: 119 kcal, Carbs: 20 g, Fat: 4 g. Protein: 12 g

Healthy Onion Rings

Prepping time: 10 minutes/ Cooking time: 10 minutes/ For 4 servings

Ingredients

- 1/4 teaspoon salt
- 1 egg
- 3/4 cup milk
- 1 tablespoon baking powder
- 3/4 cup breadcrumbs
- 1 large onion
- 1 cup flour
- 1 teaspoon paprika

Directions

1. Pre-heat Ninja Foodi by pressing the "AIR CRISP" option and setting it to "340 Degrees F" and timer to 10 minutes
2. let it pre-heat until you hear a beep
3. Take a bowl and whisk the egg, milk, salt, flour, paprika together
4. Slice the onion and separate into rings
5. Grease your Ninja Foodi Smart XL Grill with cooking spray
6. Then dip the onion rings into batter and coat with breadcrumbs
7. Arrange them in Ninja Foodi Smart XL Grill Cooking Basket
8. Cook for 10 minutes
9. Serve and enjoy!

Nutrition value per serving

Calories: 450 kcal, Carbs: 56 g, Fat: 13 g. Protein: 30 g

Chapter 6: Fish and Seafood Recipes

Juicy Lemon and Mustard Fish

Prepping time: 5-10 minutes/ Cooking time: 10 minutes /For 4 servings

Ingredients

- 2 fish fillets
- Salt and pepper to taste
- ½ teaspoon ground thyme
- 2 garlic cloves, minced
- 2 tablespoons olive oil
- 1 tablespoon Dijon mustard
- 2 tablespoons lemon juice

Directions

1. Take a bowl and add listed ingredients, mix well
2. Spread the mixture on top of the fish and on the sides
3. Add salmon to the crisping tray
4. Transfer crisping tray to your Ninja Foodi Smart XL, set to AIR CRISP mode
5. Air Fry for 7-10 minutes at 400 degrees F
6. Serve and enjoy once done!

Nutrition value per serving

Calories: 341, Fat: 15 g, Saturated Fat: 5 g, Carbohydrates: 3 g, Fiber: 1 g, Sodium: 372 mg, Protein: 47 g

The Cool Haddock Bake

Prepping time: 10 minutes/ Cooking time: 5-10 minutes /For 4 servings

Ingredients

- ¼ teaspoon salt
- ¾ cup breadcrumbs
- ¼ cup parmesan cheese, grated
- ¼ teaspoon ground thyme
- ¼ cup butter, melted
- 1 pound haddock fillets
- ¾ cup milk

Directions

1. Take your fish fillets and dredge them well in milk, season with salt and keep them on the side
2. Take a medium-sized mixing bowl, add thyme
3. Add parmesan, cheese, breadcrumbs and mix well
4. Coat the fillets well with the crumb mixture
5. Set your Ninja Foodi Smart XL to BAKE
6. Set temperature to 325 degrees F, set the timer to 13 minutes
7. Transfer to the appliance, cook for 8 minutes
8. Flip and cook for 8 minutes more
9. Enjoy

Nutrition value per serving

Calories: 450, Fat: 27 g, Saturated Fat: 12 g, Carbohydrates: 16 g, Fiber: 22 g, Sodium: 1056 mg, Protein: 44 g

Southern Catfish

Prepping time: 5 minutes/ Cooking time: 13 minutes /For 4 servings

Ingredients

- 1 lemon
- 2 pounds catfish fillets

CORNMEAL SEASONING MIX:

- 2 tablespoons dried parsley flakes
- ½ cup cornmeal
- ¼ cup all-purpose flour
- ¼ teaspoon chili powder
- ¼ teaspoon black pepper

- 1 cup milk
- ½ cup yellow mustard

- ¼ teaspoon cayenne pepper
- ½ teaspoon kosher salt
- ¼ teaspoon onion powder
- ¼ teaspoon garlic powder

Preparation:

1. Select the "Air Crisp" button on the Ninja Foodi Smart XL Grill and regulate the settings at 400 degrees F for 13 minutes.

2. Mingle the Catfish with milk and lemon juice and let it refrigerate for about 30 minutes.

3. Toss well the cornmeal seasoning ingredients in a bowl.

4. Pat dry the catfish fillets and scrub with mustard.

5. Coat the catfish fillets with cornmeal mixture and arrange the fillets in the Ninja Foodi when it displays "Add Food".

6. Shower with cooking oil and air crisp for about 10 minutes, tossing the fillets in between.

7. Dole out the fillets in a platter and serve warm.

Serving Suggestions: Quinoa salad will be a great choice for serving.

Variation Tip: Season the fish according to your choice.

Nutrition value per serving

Calories: 231, Fat: 20.1g, Sat Fat: 2.4g, Carbohydrates: 20.1g, Fiber: 0.9g, Sugar: 3.6g, Protein: 14.6g

Garlic and Salmon Extravaganza

Prepping time: 10 minutes/ Cooking time: 12 minutes /For 4 servings

Ingredients

- 2 salmon fillets, 6 ounces each
- 1 teaspoon lemon zest, grated
- ¼ teaspoon fresh rosemary, minced
- ¼ teaspoon salt
- 1 garlic clove, minced
- ¼ teaspoon pepper

Directions

1. Take a bowl and add listed ingredients except for salmon, mix thoroughly
2. Add salmon, let the mixture sit for 15 minutes
3. Set your Ninja Foodi Smart XL to GRILL, MED mode
4. Set timer to 6 minutes
5. Arrange the prepared salmon over the grill grate, lock, and cook for 3 minutes
6. Flip and cook for 3 minutes more
7. Serve once done and enjoy it!

Nutrition value per serving

Calories: 250, Fat: 8 g, Saturated Fat: 3g, Carbohydrates: 22 g, Fiber: 3 g, Sodium: 370 mg, Protein: 36 g

Broiled Tilapia

Prepping time: 5 minutes/ Cooking time: 8 minutes /For 2 servings

Ingredients

- Old Bay seasoning, to taste
- 1 pound tilapia fillets
- Lemon pepper, to taste
- Molly mcbutter, to taste
- Salt, to taste
- Cooking oil spray

Preparation:

1. Select the "Broil" button on the Ninja Foodi Smart XL Grill and regulate the settings for 8 minutes.

2. Brush the tilapia fillets with all the seasonings.

3. Arrange the tilapia fillets in the Ninja Foodi when it displays "Add Food" and shower with cooking oil spray.

4. Broil for about 8 minutes, tossing the fillets in between.

5. Dole out the fillets in a platter and serve warm.

Serving Suggestions: Serve the broiled tilapia with fresh baby greens.

Variation Tip: Cod can also be replaced with tilapia.

Nutrition value per serving

Calories: 192, Fat: 2.3g, Sat Fat: 1g, Carbohydrates: 0.5g, Fiber: 0g, Sugar: 0g, Protein: 42.2g

Paprika Shrimp

Prepping time: 10 minutes/ Cooking time: 15 minutes /For 3 servings

Ingredients

- Salt, to taste
- ½ teaspoon smoked paprika
- 2 tablespoons avocado oil
- 1 pound tiger shrimp

Preparation:

1. Select the "Bake" button on the Ninja Foodi Smart XL Grill and regulate the settings at Medium for 15 minutes.
2. Mingle the tiger shrimp, avocado oil, salt, and paprika in a bowl.
3. Arrange the shrimp mixture in the Ninja Foodi when it displays "Add Food".
4. Bake for about 10 minutes and dole out to serve warm.

Serving Suggestions: You can also serve topped with cayenne pepper.

Variation Tip: Avoid shrimp that smell like ammonia.

Nutrition value per serving

Calories: 173, Fat: 8.3g, Sat Fat: 1.3g, Carbohydrates: 0.1g, Fiber: 0.1g, Sugar: 0g, Protein: 23.8g

Salmon and Broccoli

Prepping time: 15 minutes/ Cooking time: 10 minutes /For 5 servings

Ingredients

- 2 garlic cloves, minced
- 1 pound salmon, chunked
- 1 tablespoon coconut aminos, gluten free
- 5 cups broccoli, chopped
- 3 scallions, thinly sliced
- 3 tablespoons olive oil
- 1 tablespoon dark sesame oil
- ¾ teaspoon red pepper flakes
- inch piece fresh ginger, minced
- Salt and black pepper, to taste

Preparation:

1. Select the "Grill" button on the Ninja Foodi Smart XL Grill and regulate the settings at Medium for 10 minutes.

2. Mingle the salmon chunks and broccoli with rest of the ingredients in a bowl.

3. Arrange the salmon mixture in the Ninja Foodi when it displays "Add Food".

4. Grill for about 10 minutes and dole out to serve warm.

Serving Suggestions: Serve topped with sesame seeds.

Variation Tip: You can also use cauliflower instead of broccoli.

Nutrition value per serving

Calories: 276, Fat: 18.3g, Sat Fat: 2.4g, Carbohydrates: 8.7g, Fiber: 3.1g, Sugar: 1.8g, Protein: 21.1g

Air Crisped Salmon

Prepping time: 5 minutes/ Cooking time: 8 minutes /For 2 servings

Ingredients

- 4 teaspoons avocado oil
- 2 salmon fillets
- 4 teaspoons paprika
- Lemon wedges
- Salt and coarse black pepper, to taste

Directions

1. Choose the "Air Crisp" button on the Ninja Foodi Smart XL Grill and regulate the settings at 390 degrees F for 8 minutes.

2. Brush the salmon fillets with avocado oil, salt, black pepper, and paprika.

3. Arrange the salmon fillets in the Ninja Foodi when it displays "Add Food".

4. Air crisp for about 8 minutes, tossing the fillets in between.

5. Dole out the fillets in a platter and serve warm.

Nutrition value per serving

Calories: 308, Fat: 20.5g, Sat Fat: 3g, Carbohydrates: 10.3g, Fiber: 4.3g, Sugar: 5.5g, Protein: 49g

Breaded Shrimp

Prepping time: 5 minutes/ Cooking time: 16 minutes /For 4 servings

Ingredients

- 1 pound shrimp, peeled and deveined
- 2 eggs
- ½ cup panko breadcrumbs
- 1 teaspoon garlic powder
- 1 teaspoon black pepper
- 1 teaspoon ginger
- ½ cup onion, peeled and diced

Preparation:

1. Select the "Air Crisp" button on the Ninja Foodi Smart XL Grill and regulate the settings at 350 degrees F for 16 minutes.
2. Mingle breadcrumbs, spices, and onions in one bowl, and whip eggs in another bowl.
3. Dip the shrimp in the whipped eggs and then dredge in the breadcrumbs mixture.
4. Arrange the shrimp in the Ninja Foodi when it displays "Add Food".
5. Grill for about 16 minutes, tossing the shrimps in between.
6. Dole out the shrimps in a platter and serve warm.

Serving Suggestions: Serve breaded shrimp with lemon butter.

Variation Tip: You can also use fresh ginger and garlic instead of powdered ginger and garlic.

Nutrition value per serving

Calories: 212, Fat: 4.4g, Sat Fat: 1.3g, Carbohydrates: 11.9g, Fiber: 1.6g, Sugar: 1.2g, Protein: 30g

Tuna Patties

Prepping time: 5 minutes/ Cooking time: 10 minutes /For 4 servings

Ingredients

- 2 cans tuna, packed in water
- 1½ tablespoons almond flour
- 1½ tablespoons mayonnaise
- Pinch of salt and pepper
- ½ teaspoon onion powder
- 1 teaspoon garlic powder
- 1 teaspoon dried dill
- ½ lemon, juiced

Preparation:

1. Select the "Grill" button on the Ninja Foodi Smart XL Grill and regulate the settings at Medium for 10 minutes.

2. Mingle all the tuna patties ingredients in a bowl and create equal-sized patties from this mixture.

3. Arrange the tuna patties in the Ninja Foodi when it displays "Add Food".

4. Grill for about 10 minutes, tossing the patties once in between.

5. Dole out the fillets in a platter and serve warm.

Serving Suggestions: Serve with the garlic mayo dip.

Variation Tip: You can also use fresh garlic instead of powdered garlic.

Nutrition value per serving

Calories: 338, Fat: 3.8g, Sat Fat: 0.7g, Carbohydrates: 8.3g, Fiber: 2.4g, Sugar: 3g, Protein: 15.4g

Excellent Clams

Prepping time: 5-10 minutes/ Cooking time: 5 minutes /For 4 servings

Ingredients

- 1 pack frozen clams
- Italian seasoning as needed

Directions

1. Preheat your Ninja Foodi Smart XL in AIR CRISP mode, setting the temperature to 400 degrees F for 5 minutes
2. Add the clams to the Crisping Tray, season them with your desired Italian seasoning mix
3. Cook for about 5 minutes
4. Make sure to check they are thoroughly cooked
5. If yes, serve
6. If not, let them cook for a few minutes more
7. Serve with lemon wedges, enjoy!

Nutrition value per serving

Calories: 233, Fat: 5 g, Saturated Fat: 2 g, Carbohydrates: 35 g, Fiber: 7 g, Sodium: 405 mg, Protein: 12 g

Crispy Healthy Crabby Patties

Prepping time: 5-10 minutes/ Cooking time: 10 minutes /For 4 servings

Ingredients

- Salt and pepper to taste
- 1 egg, beaten
- 1 lemon, zest
- 2 tablespoons almond flour
- 2 tablespoons Dijon mustard
- ¼ cup parsley, minced
- 12 ounces lump crabmeat
- ¼ cup mayonnaise, low carb
- 1 shallot, minced

Directions

1. Take a mixing bowl and add all ingredients, mix well and prepare 4 meat from the mixture

2. Preheat Ninja Foodi Smart XL by pressing the "AIR CRISP" option and setting it to "375 Degrees F" and timer to 10 minutes

3. Let it preheat until you hear a beep

4. Transfer patties to cooking basket and let them cook for 5 minutes, flip and cook for 5 minutes more

5. Serve and enjoy once done!

Nutrition value per serving

Calories: 177, Fat: 13 g, Saturated Fat: 4 g, Carbohydrates: 2.5 g, Fiber: 1 g, Sodium: 635 mg, Protein: 11 g

Butter and Garlic Shrimp

Prepping time: 5-10 minutes/ Cooking time: 5 minutes /For 4 servings

Ingredients

- 2 garlic cloves, minced
- Salt and pepper to taste
- 1 teaspoon dried parsley
- ½ cup butter, melted
- 1 pound shrimp, peeled and deveined

Directions

1. Take a bowl and add all listed ingredients except shrimp
2. Coat shrimp with the mixture well
3. Transfer to the Air Crisping basket
4. Set your Ninja Foodi Smart XL to Air Crisp mode
5. Air Fry the shrimp for 5 minutes at 400 degrees F
6. Serve and enjoy once done!

Nutrition value per serving

Calories: 159, Fat: 13 g, Saturated Fat: 5 g, Carbohydrates: 3 g, Fiber: 1 g, Sodium: 309 mg, Protein: 8 g

4 Ingredients Catfish

Prepping time: 5 minutes/ Cooking time: 12 minutes /For 4 servings

Ingredients

- 1 tablespoon parsley, chopped
- ¼ cup Louisiana fish seasoning
- 4 catfish fillets
- 1 tablespoon olive oil

Preparation:

1. Select the "Grill" button on the Ninja Foodi Smart XL Grill and regulate the settimgs at Medium for 12 minutes.

2. Mingle the catfish fillets with Louisiana fish seasoning in a bowl.

3. Arrange the fillets in the Ninja Foodi when it displays "Add Food" and shower with olive oil.

4. Grill for about 12 minutes, tossing the fillets in between.

5. Dole out the fillets in a platter and garnish with parsley to serve.

Serving Suggestions: Serve with steamed asparagus.

Variation Tip: For best result, use freshly squeezed lime juice.

Nutrition value per serving

Calories: 253, Fat: 7.5g, Sat Fat: 1.1g, Carbohydrates: 10.4g, Fiber: 0g, Sugar: 4.4g, Protein: 13.1g

Shrimp Lettuce Wraps

Prepping time: 20 minutes/ Cooking time: 10 minutes /For 10 servings

Ingredients

- 2 tablespoons extra-virgin olive oil
- 1 pound shrimps
- 2 garlic cloves, minced
- ½ cup summer squash, chopped
- 1 onion, chopped
- ½ cup zucchini, chopped
- Black pepper, to taste
- 1 green bell pepper, seeded and chopped
- ½ teaspoon curry powder
- 1 cup carrot, peeled and chopped
- 2 tablespoons low-sodium soy sauce
- 10 large lettuce leaves

Directions

1. Select the "Grill" button on the Ninja Foodi Smart XL Grill and regulate the settings at Medium for 10 minutes.
2. Mingle the shrimps with soy sauce, curry powder, vegetables, and black pepper in a bowl.
3. Arrange the shrimps mixture in the Ninja Foodi when it displays "Add Food".
4. Grill for about 10 minutes and dole out the shrimps mixture.
5. Insert the shrimp mixture over the lettuce leaves and serve.

Serving Suggestions: Enjoy the Shrimp Lettuce Wraps with grilled vegetables.

Variation Tip: You can also use mirin insteag of soy sauce.

Nutrition value per serving

Calories: 97, Fat: 3.7g, Sat Fat: 0.6g, Carbohydrates: 5.1g, Fiber: 0.9g, Sugar: 2.3g, Protein: 11.1g

Chapter 7: Vegetarian and Vegan Recipes

Spiced Up Chickpeas

Prepping time: 5-10 minutes/ Cooking time:10 minutes /For 4 servings

Ingredients

- Salt to taste
- ½ teaspoon cayenne pepper
- 1 teaspoon ground cumin
- 1 teaspoon chili powder
- 1 tablespoon olive oil
- 15 ounces chickpeas, canned, rinsed and drained

Directions

1. Take your chickpeas and coat them with oil
2. Season them well with cayenne, chili powder, cumin, pepper, and salt
3. Transfer them to Crisp Tray
4. Set your Ninja Foodi Smart XL to AIR CRISP mode, cook at 390 degrees F for 10 minutes making sure to stir once or twice
5. Serve and enjoy once done!

Nutrition value per serving

Calories: 182, Fat: 7 g, Saturated Fat: 3 g, Carbohydrates: 25 g, Fiber: 4 g, Sodium: 264 mg

Cheesy Zucchini Love

Prepping time: 5-10 minutes/ Cooking time: 8 minutes /For 4 servings

Ingredients

- 1 teaspoon olive oil
- ½ teaspoon tomato paste
- 1 zucchini
- ¼ teaspoon dried basil
- ½ teaspoon chili flakes
- 5 ounces parmesan, shredded

Directions

1. Take zucchini and cut into halves, scoop out the flesh from them, and spread tomato paste inside the halves

2. Add shredded cheese, sprinkle with chili flakes, dried basil, olive oil

3. Preheat Ninja Foodi Smart XI by pressing the "AIR CRISP" option and setting it to "375 Degrees F" and timer to 8 minutes

4. Let it preheat until you hear a beep

5. Arrange the prepared zucchini halves in Ninja Foodi Grill Basket, cook until the timer runs out

6. Serve and enjoy!

Nutrition value per serving

Calories: 300, Fat: 21 g, Saturated Fat: 1 g, Carbohydrates: 6 g, Fiber: 1 g, Sodium: 459 mg, Protein: 12 g

Hyper Garlic Potatoes

Prepping time: 5-10 minutes/ Cooking time: 20 minutes /For 4 servings

Ingredients

- ½ teaspoon salt
- ½ teaspoon dried parsley
- ¼ teaspoon fresh ground black pepper
- ¼ teaspoon celery powder
- ½ teaspoon garlic powder
- ½ teaspoon onion powder
- ¼ cup dried onion flakes
- 2 tablespoons extra virgin olive oil
- 2 pounds baby red potatoes, quartered

Directions

1. Take a large bowl and add all listed ingredients, toss well and coat them well
2. Preheat Ninja Foodi Smart XL by pressing the "AIR CRISP" option and setting it to "390 Degrees F" and timer to 20 minutes
3. let it preheat until you hear a beep
4. Once preheated, add potatoes to the cooking basket
5. Lock and cook for 10 minutes, making sure to shake the basket and cook for 10 minutes more
6. Once done, check the crispiness; if it's alright, serve away.
7. If not, cook for 5 minutes more
8. Enjoy!

Nutrition value per serving

Calories: 232, Fat: 39 g, Saturated Fat: 7 g, Carbohydrates: 39 g, Fiber: 5 g, Sodium: 485 mg, Protein: 4 g

Fancy Asparagus and Roasted Potatoes

Prepping time: 5-10 minutes/ Cooking time: 10 minutes /For 4 servings

Ingredients

- Salt and pepper to taste
- 1 teaspoon dried dill
- 4 potatoes, diced and boiled
- 2 stalks scallions, chopped
- 1 tablespoon olive oil
- 1 pound asparagus, trimmed and sliced

Directions

1. Take the asparagus and coat with oil
2. Season well with scallions
3. Set your Ninja Foodi Smart XL to AIR CRISP mode and set the temperature to 350 degrees F; set timer to 5 minutes
4. Once done, transfer asparagus to the cooking basket, cook for 5 minutes
5. Transfer to a bowl
6. Stir in remaining ingredients and mix well
7. Serve and enjoy!

Nutrition value per serving

Calories: 222, Fat: 8 g, Saturated Fat: 3 g, Carbohydrates: 36 g, Fiber: 3 g, Sodium: 779 mg, Protein: 6 g

Mexican Corn Dish

Prepping time: 5-10 minutes/ Cooking time: 12 minutes /For 4 servings

Ingredients

- 2 tablespoons lime juice
- ½ cup mayonnaise
- ½ cup sour cream
- 2 teaspoons garlic powder
- 2 teaspoons onion powder
- 1 and ¼ cups Cotija cheese, crumbled
- Salt and pepper to taste
- 3 tablespoons canola oil
- 6 ears corn

Directions

1. Set your Ninja Foodi Smart XL to grill mode, set temperature to MAX, and timer to 12 minutes
2. Let it preheat until you hear a beep
3. Brush the corn ears with oil, season with salt and pepper
4. Transfer to grill and cook for 6 minutes per side
5. Take a bowl and mix in the remaining ingredients; mix well
6. Cover corn mix and serve
7. Enjoy!

Nutrition value per serving

Calories: 156, Fat: 10 g, Saturated Fat: 3 g, Carbohydrates: 15 g, Fiber: 3 g, Sodium: 163 mg, Protein: 6 g

Tomatoes Balsamic Roast

Prepping time: 5-10 minutes/ Cooking time: 5 minutes /For 4 servings

Ingredients

- 1 teaspoon Italian seasoning
- ½ cup balsamic vinegar
- 1 pound tomatoes, sliced into quarters

Directions

1. Take your tomatoes and toss them well in vinegar
2. Season them with Italian seasoning
3. Transfer to Air Crisping basket
4. Set your Ninja Foodi Smart XL to Air Crisp mode
5. Set the temperature to 350 degrees F, and set the timer to 5 minutes
6. Transfer Brussels to the cooking basket, cook until done
7. Serve and enjoy!

Nutrition value per serving

Calories: 174, Fat: 14 g, Saturated Fat: 3 g, Carbohydrates: 12 g, Fiber: 2 g, Sodium: 11 mg, Protein: 2 g

Lemon Pepper Brussels Sprouts

Prepping time: 5-10 minutes/ Cooking time: 10 minutes /For 4 servings

Ingredients

- Salt to taste
- 2 teaspoons lemon pepper seasoning
- 2 tablespoons olive oil
- 1 pound brussels sprouts, sliced

Directions

1. Take your Brussels and coat them with oil

2. Season the sprouts with salt and lemon pepper

3. Spread the prepared Brussels over the Cooking basket

4. Select the broil option, with the temperature set to 350 degrees F and timer set to 5 minutes

5. Let it cook, serve, and enjoy!

Nutrition value per serving

Calories: 229, Fat: 18 g, Saturated Fat: 2 g, Carbohydrates: 12 g, Fiber: 2 g, Sodium: 360 mg, Protein: 8 g

Spicy Broccoli Medley

Prepping time: 5-10 minutes/ Cooking time: 15 minutes /For 4 servings

Ingredients

- ½ teaspoon red pepper flakes
- ¼ cup toasted almonds, sliced
- 1 large broccoli head, cut into florets
- 2 tablespoons extra virgin olive oil
- Salt and pepper to taste
- 2 tablespoons parmesan, grated
- Lemon wedges

Directions

1. Take a mixing bowl, add broccoli and toss with olive oil. Season with salt and pepper. Add red pepper flakes and toss well

2. Preheat Ninja Foodi Smart XL by pressing the "AIR CRISP" option and setting it to "390 Degrees F" and timer to 15 minutes

3. Let it preheat until you hear a beep

4. Arrange a reversible trivet in the Grill Pan, arrange broccoli crisps in the trivet

5. Let them roast until the timer runs out

6. Serve and enjoy with cheese on top and some lemon wedges!

Nutrition value per serving

Calories: 181, Fat: 11 g, Saturated Fat: 3 g, Carbohydrates: 9 g, Fiber: 4 g, Sodium: 421 mg, Protein: 8 g

Feisty Avocado Toast

Prepping time: 5-10 minutes/ Cooking time: 5 minutes /For 2 servings

Ingredients

- ¼ cup tomato, chopped
- 2 slices bread
- Salt to taste
- 1 teaspoon lemon juice
- 1 garlic clove, minced
- 1 avocado, mashed

Directions

1. Take a bowl and add avocado, lemon juice, garlic, salt, and pepper
2. Spread the mix over bread slices
3. Sprinkle tomato on top
4. Transfer to the Ninja Foodi Smart XL and grill for 2-3 minutes at 350 degrees F on GRILL mode
5. Serve and enjoy!

Nutrition value per serving

Calories: 226, Fat: 15 g, Saturated Fat: 3 g, Carbohydrates: 21 g, Fiber: 2 g, Sodium: 267 mg, Protein: 5 g

Chapter 8: Desserts Recipes

Grilled Honey Carrots

Prepping time: 15 minutes/ Cooking time: 10 minutes/ For 4 servings

Ingredients

- 6 carrots, peeled and cut lengthwise
- 2 tablespoons butter, melted
- 1 tablespoon honey
- 1 tablespoon parsley, chopped
- 1 tablespoon rosemary, chopped
- 1 teaspoon kosher salt

Directions

1. Take a ninja foodi grill, arrange it over kitchen platform
2. Arrange the grill grate and close the lid
3. Pre-heat Ninja Foodi by pressing the "GRILL" option and setting it to "MED" and timer to 10 minutes
4. Let it pre-heat until you hear a beep
5. Arrange the carrots slices over the grill grate, lock lid and cook for 5 minutes
6. Flip them and close the lid, cook for 5 minutes more
7. Serve warm and enjoy!

Nutrition value per serving

Calories: 82 kcal, Carbs: 9.5 g, Fat: 4 g. Protein: 0.5 g

Amazing Fried Tomatoes

Prepping time: 10 minutes/ Cooking time: 5 minutes / For 4 servings

Ingredients

- 1 green tomato
- 1/4 tablespoon Creole seasoning
- Salt and pepper to taste
- 1/4 cup almond flour
- 1/4 cup buttermilk
- Bread crumbs as needed

Directions

1. Pre-heat Ninja Foodi by pressing the "AIR CRISP" option and setting it to "400 Degrees F" and timer to 5 minutes
2. let it pre-heat until you hear a beep
3. Add flour to your plate and take another plate and add buttermilk
4. Cut tomatoes and season with salt and pepper
5. Make a mix of creole seasoning and crumbs
6. Take tomato slice and cover with flour, place in buttermilk and then into crumbs
7. Repeat with all tomatoes
8. Cook the tomato slices for 5 minutes
9. Serve with basil and enjoy!

Nutrition value per serving

Calories: 200kcal, Carbs: 11 g, Fat: 12 g. Protein: 3 g

Cheesed Up Cauliflower Steak

Prepping time: 10 minutes/ Cooking time: 15 minutes/ For 4 servings

Ingredients

- 1 head cauliflower, stemmed and leaves removed
- 1/4 cup canola oil
- 1/2 teaspoon garlic powder
- 1/2 teaspoon paprika
- Salt and pepper to taste
- 1 cup cheddar cheese, shredded
- Ranch dressing, garnish
- 4 slices bacon, cooked and crumbled
- 2 tablespoons chopped fresh chives

Directions

1. Cut cauliflower from top to bottom into 2-inch steaks, reserve the remaining cauliflower to cook
2. Take a small-sized bowl and whisk in oil, garlic powder, paprika, season with salt and pepper
3. Brush each steak with oil mixture on both sides
4. Pre-heat Ninja Foodi by pressing the "GRILL" option and setting it to "MAX" and timer to 15 minutes
5. let it pre-heat until you hear a beep
6. Transfer steaks to Grill Grate, lock lid and grill for 10 minutes
7. After 10 minutes, flip steaks and top with 1/2 cup cheese
8. Lock lid and cook for 5 minutes more
9. Once done, drizzle with ranch dressing, top with bacon and chives
10. Enjoy!

Nutrition value per serving

Calories: 720 kcal, Carbs: 11 g, Fat: 19 g. Protein: 32 g

Cherry Choco Bars

Prepping time: 5 minutes/ Cooking time: 15 minutes / For 8 servings

Ingredients

- 2 cups oats
- 2 tablespoons coconut oil
- 1/2 cup almonds, sliced
- 1/2 cup chia seeds
- 1/2 cup dark chocolate, chopped
- 1/2 cup cherries, dried and chopped
- 1/2 cup prunes, pureed
- 1/2 cup quinoa, cooked
- 3/4 cup almond butter
- 1/3 cup honey
- 1/4 teaspoon salt

Directions

1. Insert the crisper basket and close the hood
2. Pre-heat Ninja Foodi by pressing the "AIR CRISP" option and setting it to 375 degrees F for 15 minutes
3. Take a mixing bowl and combine the oats, chia seeds, almonds, quinoa, cherries and chocolate
4. Take a saucepan and heat the butter, honey and coconut oil
5. Pour butter mixture over dry mixture, add salt and prunes
6. Mix until well combined
7. Take a baking dish that fits inside the air fryer
8. Cook for 15 minutes
9. Serve and enjoy!

Nutrition value per serving

Calories: 330kcal, Carbs: 35 g, Fat: 15 g. Protein: 7 g

Amazing Blueberry Cobbler

Prepping time: 10 minutes/ Cooking time: 30 minutes/ For 4 servings

Ingredients

- 4 cups fresh blueberries
- 1 teaspoon lemon zest, grated
- 1 cup sugar + 2 tablespoons
- 1 cup all-purpose flour + 2 tablespoons extra
- 1 lemon, juiced
- 2 teaspoons baking powder
- 1/4 teaspoon salt
- 6 tablespoons unsalted butter
- 3/4 cup whole milk
- 1/8 teaspoon ground cinnamon

Directions

1. Take a medium-sized bowl, add blueberries, lemon zest, 2 tablespoons sugar, 2 tablespoons flour and remaining lemon juice

2. Take a medium-sized bowl and add remaining 1 cup flour, 1 cup sugar, baking powder, salt. Cut butter into flour mixture until it forms an even crumb texture, stir in milk until you have a nice dough

3. Pre-heat Ninja Foodi by pressing the "BAKE" option and setting it to "350 Degrees F" and timer to 30 minutes

4. let it pre-heat until you hear a beep

5. Take your multi-purpose pan and pour the blueberry mixture, spread evenly well

6. Pour batter over blueberry mixture, sprinkle cinnamon over top

7. Once done, transfer pan to your Grill and lock lid, bake for 30 minutes

8. Serve once done

9. Enjoy!

Nutrition value per serving

Calories: 405 kcal, Carbs: 72 g, Fat: 13 g. Protein: 5 g

Corn Bread Biscuits

Prepping time: 10 minutes/ Cooking time: 15-20 minutes / For 4 servings

Ingredients

- 1 and 1/2 cups all-purpose flour, plus more
- 1/2 cup yellow cornmeal
- 2 and 1/2 teaspoons baking powder
- 1/2 teaspoon salt
- 1/3 cup vegetable shortening
- 2/3 cup buttermilk

Directions

1. Take a large-sized bowl and add flour, cornmeal, baking powder, salt

2. Add shortening, cut into flour mixture until well combined and the dough resembles a fine coarse meal

3. Add buttermilk and stir well until moist

4. Pre-heat Ninja Foodi by pressing the "AIR CRISP" option and setting it to "350 Degrees F" and timer to 15 minutes

5. let it pre-heat until you hear a beep

6. Once done, dust a clean work surface with flour, knead mixture on a floured surface until cohesive dough forms

7. Roll out dough to an even thickness, cut with a 2-inch biscuit cutter

8. Take your crisper basket and grease well, place 6-8 biscuits in the basket

9. Transfer to Grill and bake for 12-15 minutes until golden brown

10. Remove biscuits from the basket and repeat with remaining dough

11. Serve and enjoy!

Nutrition value per serving

Calories: 265 kcal, Carbs: 34 g, Fat: 12 g. Protein: 5 g

Feisty Rum and Pineapple Sundae

Prepping time: 10 minutes/ Cooking time: 8 minutes/ For 4 servings

Ingredients

- 1/2 cup dark rum
- 1/2 cup packed brown sugar
- 1 teaspoon ground cinnamon, plus more for garnish
- 1 pineapple cored and sliced
- Vanilla ice cream, for serving

Directions

1. Take a large-sized bowl and add rum, sugar, cinnamon

2. Add pineapple slices, arrange them in the layer. Coat mixture then let them soak for 5 minutes, per side

3. Pre-heat Ninja Foodi by pressing the "GRILL" option and setting it to "MAX" and timer to 8 minutes

4. let it pre-heat until you hear a beep

5. Strain extra rum sauce from pineapple

6. Transfer prepared fruit in grill grate in a single layer, press down fruit and lock lid

7. Grill for 6-8 minutes without flipping, work in batches if needed

8. Once done, remove and top each pineapple ring with a scoop of ice cream, sprinkle cinnamon and serve

9. Enjoy!

Nutrition value per serving

Calories: 240 kcal, Carbs: 43 g, Fat: 4 g. Protein: 2 g

Marshmallow and Banana Boats

Prepping time: 19 minutes/ Cooking time: 6 minutes / For 4 servings

Ingredients

- 4 ripe bananas
- 1 cup mini marshmallows
- 1/2 cup of chocolate chips
- 1/2 cup peanut butter chips

Directions

1. Slice a banana lengthwise, keeping its peel. Make sure to not cut all the way through

2. Use your hands to open banana peel like a book, revealing the inside of a banana

3. Divide marshmallow, chocolate chips, peanut butter among bananas, stuffing them inside

4. Pre-heat Ninja Foodi by pressing the "GRILL" option and setting it to "MEDIUM" and timer to 6 minutes

5. let it pre-heat until you hear a beep

6. Transfer banana to Grill Grate and lock lid, cook for 4-6 minutes until chocolate melts and bananas are toasted

7. Serve and enjoy!

Nutrition value per serving

Calories: 505kcal, Carbs: 82 g, Fat: 18 g. Protein: 10 g

Blueberry Lemon Muffins

Prepping time: 5 minutes/ Cooking time: 10 minutes / For 12 servings

Ingredients

- 2 and 1/2 cup of almond flour
- 1 teaspoon vanilla
- 1 lemon juice
- 2 eggs
- 1 cup blueberries
- 1/2 cup cream
- 1/4 cup avocado oil
- 1/2 cup monk fruit

Directions

1. Mix monk fruit and flour

2. Take another bowl, mix vanilla, lemon juice, cream, and eggs

3. Add mixtures together and blend well

4. Spoon batter into cupcake holders

5. Pre-heat Ninja Foodi by pressing the "BAKE" option and setting it to 320 degrees F for 6 minutes

6. Serve and enjoy!

Nutrition value per serving

Calories: 317kcal, Carbs: 40 g, Fat: 11 g. Protein: 3 g

Baked Apple

Prepping time: 5 minutes/ Cooking time: 20 minutes / For 4 servings

Ingredients

- 1 medium apple
- 2 tablespoons walnuts, chopped
- 1/4 cup of water
- 1/4 teaspoon nutmeg
- 1/4 teaspoon cinnamon
- 1 and 1/2 teaspoon ghee, melted
- 2 tablespoons raisins

Directions

1. Insert the crisper basket and close the hood

2. Pre-heat Ninja Foodi by pressing the "AIR CRISP" option and setting it to 350 degrees F for 20 minutes

3. Slice the apple in half and discard some of the flesh from the center

4. Place the frying pan

5. Take remaining ingredients together except water

6. Spoon mixture to the middle of the apple halves

7. Bake for 2o minutes

8. Serve and enjoy!

Nutrition value per serving

Calories: 205kcal, Carbs: 39 g, Fat: 11 g. Protein: 2 g

Fruity Lime Salad

Prepping time: 10 minutes/ Cooking time: 4 minutes / For 2 servings

Ingredients

- 1/2 pound strawberries washed, hulled and halved
- 1 can (9 ounces) pineapple chunks, drained, juice reserved
- 2 peaches, pitted and sliced
- 6 tablespoons honey, divided
- 1 tablespoon freshly squeezed lime juice

Directions

1. Take a large bowl and add strawberries, pineapple, peaches, and 3 tablespoons, honey, toss well

2. Pre-heat Ninja Foodi by pressing the "GRILL" option and setting it to "MAX" and timer to 4 minutes

3. Let it pre-heat until you hear a beep

4. Transfer fruits to Grill Grate, lock lid and cook for 4 minutes

5. Take a small-sized bowl and add remaining 3 tablespoons of honey, lime juice, 1 tablespoon reserved pineapple juice

6. Once cooking is done, place fruits in a large-sized bowl and toss with honey mixture, serve and enjoy!

Nutrition value per serving

Calories: 178kcal, Carbs: 47 g, Fat: 1 g. Protein: 2 g

Banana Fritter

Prepping time: 10 minutes/ Cooking time: 15 minutes / For 6 servings

Ingredients

- 1 medium butternut squash
- 2 teaspoons cumin seeds
- 1 large pinch chili flakes
- 1 tablespoon olive oil
- 1 and 1/2 ounces pine nuts
- 1 small bunch fresh coriander, chopped

Directions

1. Pre-heat Ninja Foodi by pressing the "AIR CRISP" option and setting it to "340 Degrees F" and timer to 16 minutes

2. let it pre-heat until you hear a beep

3. Take a bowl and add salt, sesame seeds, water and mix them well until a nice batter form

4. Coat the bananas with the flour mixture and transfer them to the Ninja Foodi Smart XL Grill Basket

5. Cook for 8 minutes

6. Enjoy!

Nutrition value per serving

Calories: 240 kcal, Carbs: 30 g, Fat: 10 g. Protein: 5 g

Mozzarella Sticks and Grilled Eggplant

Prepping time: 10 minutes/ Cooking time: 15 minutes/ For 4 servings

Ingredients

- 1 eggplant, sliced and 1/4 inch thick
- 2 tablespoons canola oil
- 2 heirloom tomatoes, sliced into 1/4 inch thick
- 12 large basil leaves
- 1/2 pound buffalo mozzarella, sliced into 1/4 inch thick
- Salt to taste

Directions

1. Take a large-sized bowl and add eggplant, oil and toss well

2. Pre-heat Ninja Foodi by pressing the "GRILL" option and setting it to "MAX" and timer to 15 minutes

3. let it pre-heat until you hear a beep

4. Transfer eggplants to Grill Plant, lock lid and cook for 8-12 minutes until charred well

5. After 8-12 minutes, top eggplant with one slice of tomato and mozzarella. Lock lid and cook for 2 minutes more until cheese melts

6. Once done, remove eggplant from the grill, place 2-3 basil leaves on top of half stack, place remaining eggplant stacks on top with basil

7. Season with salt, garnish with remaining basil

8. Serve and enjoy!

Nutrition value per serving

Calories: 256 kcal, Carbs: 11 g, Fat: 19 g. Protein: 32 g

Granola Muffins

Prepping time: 10 minutes/ Cooking time: 15-20 minutes / For 4 servings

Ingredients

- 3 ounces plain granola
- 3 handful of cooked vegetables of your choice
- 1/4 cup of coconut milk
- A handful of thyme diced
- 1 tablespoon coriander
- Salt and pepper to taste

Directions

1. Pre-heat Ninja Foodi by pressing the "AIR CRISP" option and setting it to "352 Degrees F" and timer to 20 minutes

2. Take a mixing bowl and add cooked vegetables

3. Take an immersion blender and whiz granola until you have a breadcrumb-like texture

4. Add coconut milk to the granola and add veggies

5. Mix well into muffin/ball shapes

6. Transfer them to pre-heated Ninja Foodi Smart XL Grill and cook for 20 minutes

7. Serve and enjoy once done!

Nutrition value per serving

Calories: 140 kcal, Carbs: 14 g, Fat: 10 g. Protein: 2 g

Cinnamon Sugar Roasted Chickpeas

Prepping time: 5 minutes/ Cooking time: 10 minutes / For 2 servings

Ingredients

- 1 tablespoon sweetener
- 1 tablespoon cinnamon
- 1 cup chickpeas
- medium apple
- 2 tablespoons walnuts, chopped
- 1/4 cup of water
- 1/4 teaspoon nutmeg
- 1/4 teaspoon cinnamon
- 1 and 1/2 teaspoon ghee, melted
- 2 tablespoons raisins

Directions

1. Insert the crisper basket and close the hood

2. Pre-heat Ninja Foodi by pressing the "AIR CRISP" option and setting it to 390 degrees F for 10 minutes

3. Rinse and drain chickpeas

4. Mix all ingredients

5. Add to air fry and cook for 10 minutes

6. Serve and enjoy!

Nutrition value per serving

Calories: 115kcal, Carbs: 25 g, Fat: 20 g. Protein: 18 g

www.ingramcontent.com/pod-product-compliance
Lightning Source LLC
Chambersburg PA
CBHW080607170426
43209CB00007B/1359